Princess Diana's Message of Peace

An Extraordinary Message of Peace
for our Current World

Channeled by Marcia McMahon

Library of Congress Control Number: 2003100322

Princess Diana's Message of Peace
An Extraordinary Message of Peace for Our Current World / McMahon 1953-

ISBN 13:978-0-9766477-1-3
ISBN 10: 0-9766477-1-0

Cover art by: Marcia McMahon

Printed in the United States of America

Eternal Rose Publishing

Address all inquiries:

You can visit Marcia's Website by going to:
www.dianaspeakstotheworld.com

This book is for ***Princess Diana,***
and
Your Children, and Your Children's Children.

It is a testament to eternal life and peace, for the good name of Princess Diana, her many good causes begun on Earth, and now continued from Heaven.

*"Let There Be Peace on Earth and Let it Begin With Me!"**

*Words and music by Sy Miller and Jill Jackson - 1955

Author’s Note:

Princess Diana's Message of Peace is a channeled work of non-fiction. The author assumes no liability for the messages from Princess Diana herein, as they are given to the author in inner dictation. The author has the ability to hear Diana's words accurately and write them as she receives them, but she cannot assume personal liability for any possible discrepancies in Diana's words or her many other biographies. She also assumes no personal liability in Diana's political views or perspectives from the afterlife.

The author believes Diana's words from the Heavenly realm are genuine and true. Furthermore, these messages are not intended to reflect in any way on the Royal Family. It is intended that the reader always read the information with an open mind and heart, and then decide through discernment what is true for oneself.

Acknowledgements

I wish here to acknowledge some of the people who have helped me immeasurably in my work on this book and the web site,

Diana Speaks to the World, at

www.dianaspeakstotheworld.com.

I wish to thank my dear friends A. and M. who choose to remain anonymous. Without their help, I could never have put together the beautiful web site. I wish to thank Dennis, my husband, for running to Capital Blueprint to pick up art work so many times. And my thanks to Rich, at Capital Blueprint for the beautiful scans of Diana's paintings. I gratefully acknowledge my family, the McMahon's in that they were in attendance at Diana's Funeral, and provided the wonderful pictures of flowers, testimonials and crowds for her sad day. I also thank Jim Wilson for his funeral pictures and support of my message.

I thank Jan Benner, my friend and healer, who has seen Princess Diana, and acknowledged Diana's presence in my life and supported my efforts. I thank Betty, a dear friend who stood by me. I thank Rev. Rita Pugh, who told me last year she saw the beautiful Angel Diana standing with me in the light, and who said that the message would be global and have a wonderful impact on people everywhere. She also acknowledged Mother Teresa holding a candle of light with Diana, who is with Diana in the peace effort.

I thank Dorothy May Mercer of Mercer Publications for her exceptional talent and efforts in editing and re-publishing this second printing of Princess Diana's Message of Peace.

I wish to acknowledge Patrick, a psychic medium who saw Diana standing with Mother Teresa behind me, at a church gathering, before we were formally introduced! Finally, I thank author Robert Murray who is also a channel for Princess Diana, (**www.TheStarsStillShine.com**) and his son James Murray, who illustrates his wonderful book on the afterlife (*The Stars Still Shine: An Afterlife Journey.*) They have been a source of inspiration and joy in sending their messages from Diana and Michael, who confirm my connection to Princess Diana, without a doubt! Thank you again, James and Bob Murray!

Most of all, I wish to thank Princess Diana, my dearest friend in spirit, for her endless hours of consultation and support in putting this book to form, and her inspiring words for our world!

Blessings to all,
Marcia McMahon
Author, artist, channel, teacher

TABLE OF CONTENTS

Prelude

What is Channeling and How Mine Began Diana's Messages

The material for a book came through me from Princess Diana in the beginning of May of 2001. I had been very ill with walking pneumonia, and as I lay in bed, I became aware of a loving presence in my room. I had been reading *The Celestial Voice of Diana; Her Guidance to Finding Love*, by Rita Eide a Norwegian channel for Diana. This loving energy was tall and blond, with an unmistakable energy of Princess Diana. Diana came to me there as I lay there quite ill and said to me, "I'm here to assist you, Darling! Just call on me, whenever you need me and I'll be there in an instant!" Unmistakably, I knew I had heard from Diana as I heard her words! I saw her standing near my bedside, and she seemed to be dressed in a black evening gown. I was not running a fever nor was I hallucinating. I was sure it was Diana. The beautiful energy I felt that evening was silken and moved with the same grace as the person we had known as Princess Diana. She waved her hands over me, and said she was going to do some healing. I lay there allowing the graceful movements of her hands over my head. I did not actually see her in full; the impression was more of an energy of her, much like a [1]

[1] Eide, Rita. *The Celestial Voice of Diana, Her Spiritual Buidance to Finding Love.* Findhorn Press, 1999, The Park, Findhorn Forres IV363TY Scotland UK

negative to a photo. So it was then, when I was in trouble with illness, that we met, and she assisted in my healing. It still took me a month more to totally recover from pneumonia. I felt very grateful and blessed by Diana for assisting in my healing, and wondered if I'd hear from her again. It was May, in the Spring when I heard these words from Diana, "You are to be an ambassador for peace in your part of the world, on my behalf."

This was actually in May of 2001. I carefully penned that into my journal. Of course I was delighted, totally flabbergasted and didn't have any idea what she meant. Of course, I said yes to her request, and I don't know if I'll ever live up to those words!

In July, she dictated her loving and supportive letters to William and Harry in my living room. It began as an inaudible inner dictation, which I recorded in my journal. For a long time I wondered what to do with those letters, and if there would be more forthcoming. I posted them on the web site and included them in the book here because they help to explain the process and relationship which I now share with Princess Diana. I debated about publishing them here, since I know that William and Harry deserve as much privacy as possible. In the long run, I felt it best that they see these letters, even though I did send them on to St. James Palace. Just because I sent these letters onward to William and Harry, doesn't mean they were received or read. As you may be aware quite a lot of the mail that comes there is read and censored. Now I believe in my heart, they reached the boys, but in the event that a palace courtier thought it in their best judgment not to give it to William or Harry, I decided to place the letters in the book and to do so in the name of Diana's motherly love for the her sons' sake. I know Diana will understand, and I certainly hope the Royal Family will understand my reasoning here. That being said, let it be said here and now that this book is not intended to reflect in any way upon the private lives of the Royal Family, and I have taken great pains to eliminate any material in the original manuscript which may have mentioned them at all! I must say for the record, Diana never speaks of them, and so it isn't really an issue. She is always most gracious whenever she mentions any of her former family, and always speaks with the greatest care for them. Diana was one year divorced before her tragic accident in the Paris tunnel, and she was well on her way to making a new life for herself. She is therefore speaking as Diana, her own person, and not at all representing the Royal Family from whom she was separated at her untimely death. Diana and I commenced the beginning of her book, which was to deal with the education of children in the new millennium, but then the tragic events of September 11th ensued. This message from Diana is about world politics and peacemaking in the new millennium with an emphasis on saving the lives of children worldwide. Since Diana was formally divorced before her tragic accident, she really was in a formal way, already very much on her own, leading a new life. It is in this spirit of world issues, which she had only begun with Land mines and her World Wide Alert against them, where this interesting book resumes Diana's causes. She has commented on Land mines and other causes of hers in this book and in *Princess Diana's Message of Peace, Book II.*

Everything changed on September 11, 2001 for all of us, collectively. Naturally, Diana's channeled messages became much more political in tone. Diana had said I was to be an ambassador for peace, for my part of the world. I had no idea until September 11th what this might now involve. In her opening sentence, Diana said that political and social stresses exist, and they will be something to contend with in the days ahead.

Channeling is quite simple and direct for me. It is like automatic writing, the words are given as I sit at my computer or write in my journal. I am fully conscious as I write, and do not enter a trance state. To do so would not allow the conversational quality of the channeled messages. To put it simply, Diana's words flow through me! I sometimes have an inner, inaudible voice and at other times I am just taking down quick dictation in words as they flow through me from Diana.

I edit proper names and spelling and adjust word syntax, but everything that comes to me is exactly as Diana words it. I do not participate in séances, or do readings for people from the spirit side, though I have from time to time given Diana's words to someone as she requests it. It seems a very natural gift although I realize I am very honored to hear from Princess Diana. She is as lovely a person in spirit, as she was in life. She is kind, thoughtful and has the interest of the world's children at heart in this book. Her heart is pure and loving, just as she was. Her beauty and eloquence in these messages is incomparable.

In my paintings of Diana, I have tried to recapture her radiance and beauty as she was, while adding a spiritual dimension to her now. I count Diana my closest and truest friend in spirit!

I am very blessed with a friend like this and so are you, the reader, blessed by her intervention into human affairs. She was a very lovely person on earth and she continues her causes from the heavens. Her message is so typically Diana; her causes are those who are suffering (the AIDS crisis in Africa, see Diana; Mother Essence for the Children of Earth) and the future of our children, especially those underprivileged children in third world countries. Her causes continue with world peace and prevention of all out world war, and especially politics in the Middle East. Yet there is something unique about this channeled material from Diana. Diana shares her unique spiritual wealth of information from her heavenly dimension now- insights into the afterlife, the order of universe, other universes, higher beings, saints, ascended masters, and God. She speaks in plain English, and she is still recognizable as **"Queen of Hearts."**

Marcia McMahon

Channeling Princess Diana

Never before in our collective spiritual history have we seen so much channeled information from higher realms. In my life, first it was *A Course in Miracles*, channeled by Jesus through Helen Schuckman and Bill Thetford. This was a mind boggling experience for me, which seemed to lead me into despair. That being said, *A Course in Miracles* laid the groundwork for me in my current channeled work with Diana, Princess of Wales. What is unique about Diana is that she is recently departed, and her messages aren't vague references to peace and love and the universe; although they do contain that. They are directions for the diplomats currently active in our tense political world. This is the exception rather than the rule with regards to channeled material. Most people who channel receive information from higher dimensional beings with the name Sananda or something. Usually these channeled messages are from advanced spirit guides, and have a sort of ring to them. Diana is straightforward, direct and urgent in her Plea for Peace, for instance, where she lays it on the line with regards the possibility for outright World War. She has spelled it out in plain English what the possible worlds scenarios are for nuclear annihilation. She highly recommends a Peace Accord in the Middle East, with Peacekeepers in the region and possible solutions which could effectively end the war on terror, and bring about total peace for humanity at this time of crisis! Angel Diana is in heaven busy dictating through me what the next political move in the Middle East should be on behalf of world peace.

In the many documentaries on Princess Diana that have aired, the BBC ran one on the Life of Diana around the time of her death, August 31st, 2001. I distinctly remember an interview she held with a reporter (while she was on a walkabout in Britain) when she was asked what she'd like to be if she could be anything other than Princess of Wales. She overwhelmingly replied "I'd like to be Ambassador for Britain!" This she claims in her message dated October 6, 2001 in her Plea for Prayer and Peace, where she states that she held a friendship with Tony Blair and he had already appointed her Ambassador for Britain. In this, I take it to mean she held an unofficial position of Goodwill Ambassador, certainly not representing the Royal Family or the Crown, but certainly representing goodwill everywhere in the world!

This is the thrust this book has taken, with Diana as a guide through one of our country's and world's most devastating events and most critical times. She references certain diplomats, Colin Powell in particular, to whom these messages seem written. She also references Mr. Tony Blair, Mr. Kofi Annan, and Mr. George Bush. She asked me to research her contacts in diplomats she had known and write to each one.

Diana, Princess of Love, has changed the world again! This time, not with her marriage to a Prince (Charles), or the birth of her two beautiful sons, or even her tragic death which opened us like nothing had. This time, it is Diana's most poignant voice of Love calling from the unknown heavens to the known, for us, "to make peace here, for our children, and our children's children!"

Diana, the Princess, bows to the peace workers, Colin Powell, Kofi Annan and all the others she refers to. In truth, she is doing this work from her heavenly office, where she need no longer worry about the impact that the Palace is having on her work. She seldom if ever speaks of the Royal

Family and prefers privacy for them. She does speak very lovingly of her two sons William and Harry and her love and devotion to them, which will continue forever.(See Diana's Letter to William, and Diana's Letter to Harry.) She also sends her love on to the celebrities she knew in life: Elton John is referred to more than once, and she mentions both John Lennon and George Harrison as being with her in spirit from time to time.

She speaks on the world-wide plight of children and starvation, AIDS in Africa, and possible weather catastrophes, and all her causes come with Diana on the side of the underprivileged. She calls herself "Diana, Heartbeat of the Mother Essence for the Children of the World," see Diana, Mother Comfort, painting by the author, or go to the web site to view this painting.

Of course, she is still, world-wide, the only Princess Diana, "Queen of Hearts!" I have grown to love Princess Diana in the quiet recesses of my heart and mind, as a trusted friend and healer, and as an Ascended Master dwelling in the highest realms of pure heaven.

All my love in Diana, Marcia McMahon Her Channel

Diana's Letter to William

My Dearest William,

July, 2001

It has been so long since my departure, dearest, I hope you think of me now and then. I want you to know that I am immensely happy here in heaven, as I also have much work here, too.

I am involved in many similar causes as I was on Earth, specifically dealing with grief and those recently passed over. Only from here, in my unique vantage point affords me greater vision.

I have come to speak to you today about your future William, which I can see from here more clearly than those on Earth. First of all William, know that you are dearly loved by your earthly mother, Diana! Know that I am by your side, in all you do! On Earth, we had to wait to see each other, but here I see so much more and am so much closer!

William, you have a very special part to play! I can't reveal all the details because that would spoil the ending of the story for you, just like when you were little! Here there is so much to both see — and do!

At the same time that you are both special and royal, you are going to understand soon the necessity of becoming One! One of the many blessed with gifts and talents, which you always had, and one with humanity as a whole. By this I mean that you are to be instrumental, by example, in continuing my humanitarian endeavor. This you knew about since when you were young. This will become increasingly important, that the world know you care as much as I do about world hunger, AIDS epidemic, and all the other causes I was involved in. For if the monarchy is to be saved at all, you, William will be reestablishing the role of shall we say, "Modern Monarch"!

Due to social stresses all over the world, many upheavals will be occurring. The consciousness of the entire planet will change in your lifetime, William. As your mother, always, I want to see you through any storm, no matter large or small. In these forthcoming events, William, I shall be with you and your brother!

At this juncture in time, the earth and all its inhabitants will be going through a transformation, unlike any seen before. So earth-shattering will this be that many will not live through it, without spiritual support. You may reference my book, *The Celestial Voice of Diana* for further details. But, you mustn't lose heart!

This transformation has already begun in the weather patterns, global warming, and other things such as world hunger, drought and so on. My message here, my beloved son, is to have hope when things look bleak. With my light, your future will be bright! You are a child of the stars, born to be a light bearer! You will help many find their light and share with so many others! So that Earth will truly be shining with a light so bright — oh, William so much good is in store for you and the whole human race!

There are turning points in your life. I know also there is much you'd like to confide in me, like we used to do. But know that whenever you need help, turn within, listen in the stillness to God. Let your choice be whatever feels right to you after you've had the chance to be alone. Oh, I know that will be hard! But if you listen to your own inner resources William, you will always make the right choice. You may turn to me in thought and to God in prayer, at these crucial times. (We are as one here on this side.)

And then you can release these decisions to the One who knows your best intentions!

William, when I died, I pleaded with God to let me return to you and your brother Harry. I couldn't bear the departure. It was explained to me there, in the 7th heaven, that my injuries were too serious, that I would have to give up my present earthly lifetime. I know how you must feel being deprived of an earthly mother, as I was. But you are not deprived! For I am eternally, your loving mother, Diana.

And in this sense I am 'eternally yours!' You can turn to me for guidance and assurance, and I can come in an instant. As I come to you in spirit now, through this channel, I come through other channels as well. Oh, William, if you knew the Heaven here, you would not grieve so much for me! My sudden departure really shook you, I know.

Everything here is just like Earth, except that we can be many places at one time, assisting many simultaneously. Oh, William if you knew my joy now, there would be no more tears my darling!

I ask you to take this letter on faith. My channel wants you to know that this is genuine truth, not mere media hype! She is being as true a listener to my voice as she presently can. If you will read my books, I think you will get further education for your new role in the new order of the world at this time. Not to replace the education you are planning, but to further it. Over here, I've learned so much from the scientists! I've been involved in classes where I further my education. (So much for my detractors back home!)

In closing then my dearly beloved, darling son, I LOVE YOU GREATLY! Call on me when you need

anything, I am always one thought away, one heartbeat away! Believe this: I shall save you every time! I am eternally, your loving mother,

Diana

Diana's Letter to Harry

June, 2001

My Dearest Harry;

It has been a long while, my little darling! Harry, I have missed you my Sweetie! "Mummy," as you affectionately called me on Earth, is in Heaven now, as you might suspect!

Here in Heaven we don't sit around listening to angels strum harps, although the music is wonderful! Mummy's quite happy and you needn't cry so!

Harry, this message is being delivered to you through a person who can hear my voice, sometimes known as a channel. This particular channel is an American, and though not royal, is like a good friend to Mummy now. You can trust her message - it is true.

I want you to know Mummy's all right. So wondrous a place it is, the seventh heaven is like no other palace we've ever lived in! And Jesus is right here with me as well. I want you to know that you're being looked after. From this vantage point, Heaven is like a giant sky, and we can see so much more on Earth. I can see all you're doing, and I know that the going hasn't been easy for you.

Therefore, now, I want to speak to you as though I am really here. Your mummy's passing is something that really upset you. But you were so brave a little boy!

Now that you're a bit older, I think I can tell you about some things you've been wondering about. First of all, I should like you to know now that my work continues in this life I'm in now. I regularly see children who are passing over and help to heal the grief. I know just how you feel, being without a mother, since I was without a mother as a little girl.

But you see, I'm here in Heaven and I visit you in your dreams; that's how you know we are still able to communicate. Here, we learn too, that there is no such thing as death for we are all part of the eternal Creator, creating forever.

At my passing, I didn't want to leave you. I even asked God directly if I had to go, since it was always you and your brother I was thinking of. But you see, it was my time. At this turning point in your life, I would like you to keep up with your studies, as it's very important. I want you to know I'm looking over your every turn in life, and I'm here to support you, my darling! (Even through every exam). If I could just wrap my arms around you again, like we used to do!

You see, all life is a precious gift, as you were to me. I know all the details of your life as you go through it, only without judgment. With complete love I see the goings on.

If you knew how tenderly I looked over your shoulder, you would never fear another thing! I want very much for you to go on with your life as best you can without my physical presence. But at the same time now, my darling, you are comforted by this little visit (in writing). I am forever your adoring mother. Hugs and kisses.

love, Mummy Diana

Princess Diana's Messages

Diana's Wisdom
Educating Children in the New Millennium

The purpose of this next book will be to bring children into the new millennium or age and therefore recreate the kind of world that is desired at this time. As many of you reading this material of mine know, time is of the essence in our troubled world today. Even as I speak these thoughts and words there are those in the world who would have it otherwise. A great deal of resistance to old thought systems; political, social and familial will arouse suspicion and be part of the great change that will shortly unfold. This is indeed natural to the process of change. If mankind is to survive, then these changes must be implemented or else there may not be an earth as we know it. It is foretold in so many of the prophecies; Nostradamus, the Bible, and others about these earth changes.

Many of you have witnessed already the weather patterns of the nineties and even now, things are not settled. It will be more of the same in all areas of the world, with a special emphasis on the coastal regions, and the possibility of the loss of life in great numbers. At the same time, I wish to remind my readers that there is a great possibility for the promised 1,000 years of peace at this time! And to think of disaster as the only possibility is wrong, for hope is always justified. I wish you to know that you are the creators of your destiny. If a number of you desire to make right the wrongs of the last 2,000 years it is totally possible now. Though other darker outcomes are always possible, it is up to you collectively to band together in one unified purpose, and take the future you've always dreamed possible, to create heaven on earth.

It is with this thought of heaven on earth that I speak, that I wish to teach those who are to be my teachers, using the money set up in my name to teach children and adults as well the principles herein. Whether you teach children or adults, the principles will remain the same, and be useful to your instruction. If you can bear with me in these pages forthcoming, specific instruction will be given to uplift and light your way to becoming the human-kind you are possible of experiencing.

It is with this intention at heart that I felt inspired to write this book, and it is my clear hope that you won't read this material and then put it on the shelf to collect dust, but to use it as a clear guide to reeducation- education of your young in particular. And to read this book simply because of my name is not the point either. As you know, I have been rather busy since my departure to the spirit realm, and here there is much work for me now. **So that if my name be used at all, think of it as a blessing returning to you all the love you have shown me when I lived as Princess Diana on Earth. For this, I am eternally grateful. With such love you gave, you deserve to have all that returned and more, so that humanity will know the great love that God has in mind for each one of you!**

My voice reaches millions now, as it did on earth, but more are paying attention to the spiritual messages being transmitted by so many- some still living, whilst others are channeling from spirit as I am through gifted channels. If some of the messages aren't to your liking, know too that all change is painful and don't dwell on those aspects of my

teaching. It is my hope in time you will come to see the wisdom herein, thereby declaring your freedom from human bondage to fear, starvation, separation, and loneliness to name just a few. I can give you the instruction, the keys as it were, and then you must unlock the door to your hearts, one by each. You have only to remember my heart of love, open to you and if you open yours, miracles can thus occur.

If humanity is to reach a collective heaven, there is much that each one will need to do in the realms of conscience, caring and seeing other's needs more clearly. If you can't see the good of all reflected in this teaching, then begin by thinking differently about what it means to be human and good to you. If you can simplify down to the basic needs of the heart, you will not err.

ALL MY LOVE, DIANA

Diana on World Peace Keeping Heaven in Your Heart

What is the point in this? What is the point in living without your basic needs met, in a harsh world that does not recognize the love that all of you are. You are so lovable, so needed in the world, yet you race around trying to amass more of this and more of that. You may wonder what the point is in this message, or whether it is genuine, which I assure you that it is. I have made my point in addressing the question of what this book's main theme will be. Will you do your part then, to bring the world into greater peace, greater harmony, greater good for all? That is a fundamental question which each of you will answer in your own heart, at your own pace, in your own time.

If you will simply read this you will then understand what needs to be remade, reshaped out of your own mind and heart, to recreate the heaven on Earth that was intended in the original and divine plan of the Father-Mother, eons ago. All of you were there then, just as you are now, though you may not have been in physical form as you are now.

If you can bring yourselves to a place of infinite peace, infinite joy, infinite abundance and light within, for just a second- imagine what that must feel like. Now, take that joy into your mind and heart, feel my joy coursing through you. This is what it was to be part of the first Paradise on Earth and as you remember, you can then bring forth this very energy.

It is today to this I wish to speak. Paradise can be yours today for you. God wants you to be happy, healthy and to have enough, both for you and your children.

(Diana, I have to speak here a little on my own. Today, as your words reached me, I went out to do the most beautiful watercolor, and experienced the most elegant of late summer days! My creation and atmosphere were so perfect! I feel if only every day could be so effortless, so elegant, so lovely! Thank you again.)

D: You are most welcome for that day. You see if you will just flow with your emotions, then there will never be a problem of what to do with your time. The joy you seek is the joy you really are.

I realize it is another matter to feel joy in oneself and then express that to those who are less than joyous around you. You realize that without the others there is no joy, and that with the others there is sometimes no joy to be found. This is how you feel at the moment, that there is grief in leaving what you currently have, and greater grief in finding the new fulfillment that is in store for you.

M: Yes, that is it, Diana. I can't seem to leave some of the good things behind.

D: Wisdom is in knowing when to discard what is no longer needed, but still listening to God within, you will always get a sense of the wisdom.

M: Before we move on I need to be able to clear this grief in my system with the school situation.

D: Good then go and take a walk in the garden, breath fresh air and inhale and exhale. Find my presence with you there.

Notes:

Sometime ago, I went for a healing treatment with a pranic healer by the name of Jan Benner. It is a combination of using energy healing / spiritual healing. With Jan, who is quite a powerful healer, this energy or light simply entered my body. At the beginning of the treatment, Jan said she saw a kind of line, swept into my heart, and it was triangle shaped, with the colors red, blue and gold. It was three dimensional. She said she only saw it with those who were very close to God. She said it was Diana's presence placed into my heart, to connect me to her, with a gold band around the heart to protect me from all harm. Apparently, there is some danger in channeling and energies are not the same. Later at the closing of our session together, Jesus, Mother Mary, and Diana appeared. Diana placed her hand on my heart, healing it. We on earth are vibrating at a lower speed, those in heaven are vibrating much faster, and the two are not compatible without an energy adjustment. It might be likened to the power bar. It gives us extra power, but at the same time, prevents overloads to our delicate systems.

Jan Benner is available online at: janbenner1@aol.com or by phone at 217-566-2645.

I can highly recommend Jan as a professional healer and one who is in touch with the higher realms of heaven, and she has granted my permission to use her name. She is booked months in advance.

D: Now to continue our discussion, I would like to comment on the healing session you received.

I was indeed present there, and my entire energy system was placed into your heart. So that at a later time, as you progress, I will be able to communicate more through you than I do at present.

As you must realize, you must keep your heart pure and clean of negative energy, which I sense is still present even today. If you will take a deep breath, I will come in and touch the energy point and remove it for you.

M: Thank you, Diana, I now feel it is gone.

D: My pleasure!

M: I am excited to channel you more, Diana.

D: Oh, and what a lovely thing it will be to receive my presence, which as you know on this plane is pure love. As you know, it is harder in the relative world to stay in the presence of pure love.

M: Is that what you mean by making every day a heaven on earth?

D: To answer an obvious question, of course! That is part of it, but not nearly the whole sum of it.

We'll get to that part of your education later in this discourse. Right now, for now and always, love is the starting point. If everyone could forget their cares and just love, so many problems would dissolve instantly.

M: Well said and speaking from the heart of love you have for humanity, I am again humbled by your presence, and by this unique assignment.

D: This book will be your greatest pleasure, and of course, mine as well. When we come to you at distinct points in time, we are able to physically enter your force field, and our vibrations will change you at this point, just as you now felt.

M: Diana, just now I felt the most peaceful, blissful presence, as though waves of love and grace we pouring over me.

D: Yes, that is how you will feel, and that is why I say that it will be a total pleasure getting to know you in this endeavor, for we become as one, even as my heartbeat beats with your heartbeat, and my energy system or vibration, overlaps yours. It is equally important to realize the teaching of Jesus the Christ who taught us so much about love, for when we are in love, everything is possible.

M: Diana, your presence is so serene, so uplifting, so true to the essence that was you, Princess Diana, on earth. I feel a little embarrassed, being so honored with not only your gracious ways and thoughts, but with your very presence.

D: And it will continue that way until the session is over. You will then begin to understand that keeping heaven within your own heart, your own energy system is the most important thing a human being can do. It surpasses all the accomplishments of a lifetime. And you have had so many, but this one will be pleasure instead of pain to you!

M: I am so graced, humbled, and honored!

D: You are receiving my healing essence right now. I want you to let go of thought, and receive it. When I am ready to speak, I will let you know.

M: I laid down for a time, and felt your healing presence. It was as if colors were entering my system, from the head and then from the feet. And my heart energy had a chance to work completely out of my system.

D: Very well then, you're happy now?

M: Delighted.

D: My pleasure. It is my greatest pleasure to share my love and healing where I can. You now see that your visit to the chiropractor wasn't necessary this time!

M: Oh, far more powerful, Diana. Thank you again.

D: You're very welcome.

M: Is that it for now or today? Did you have another topic to discuss, now that I feel all blissed out, and totally refreshed?

D: It is always my pleasure to be with you longer if you wish to continue.

M: Oh, you English, your Royal Highness have so much in the way of grace and manors!

D: As it should be.

6. **Diana's Spirit Taking Leave of Earthly Things,** (Althorp)

©2001, watercolor by Marcia McMahon

III.Diana's Spirit Taking Leave of Earthly Things (Angel of Althorp, burial place of Diana, Princess of Wales), watercolor by Marcia McMahon. Diana is laid to rest on an island in a lake owned by her family, the Spencers, known as Althorp. In the background, you can see the island with the marker where she is buried. Visible in the background is the Diana temple, a memorial for her. Althorp is open to receive visitors two months out of the year in the summer. You can reference Althorp online to buy tickets. I have yet to go there but did this painting from a photo taken by a dear friend who makes a yearly pilgrimage. To view the watercolor in color go to: www.angelfire.com/mb2/diana_speaks/gallery_index.html

Diana Gallery One, 2001.

Princess Diana's Anniversary Message August 30, 2001

M: Diana, is it your anniversary, of the time of your departure?

D: Yes, that is what I wish to speak about today.

It will have been four years since my departure from the Earth Plane. I have made strides and advances since then, as you well know. My existence here in the seventh heaven is beyond the comprehension of most. We live amongst you and in the energy grid that surrounds Earth.

We are trying to see that most of you live in peace and serenity, instead of conflict and war. While we can't do it for you, we are assisting in as many places and situations as we can. We need more channels such as you, so that the results of our teaching will be felt in the world today.

For my anniversary, I would like you to live in love in peace in my name that day. If you leave flowers and messages, I appreciate them and your love always. Remember me always in yourhearts. Do not forsake me or the lovely person I was as Princess Diana. At the same time, be aware that my transition to spirit was an appointed time, and that by using my Voice now, I can reach millions, in such a way as to reach each one. For each of your roses, I give you thanks, and return the favor to you personally. I am eternally England's Rose. I wish to be a fragrance in each heart, and a blessing to each one who calls my name. I will be there in an instant, when you call!

Honor me by being love and peace in your world for my day. I shall never forget you or forsake you!

My Love Always, Diana

Diana on the Body Centers or Chakras

M: Oh, Diana, reading this today I am welling up tears thinking of you. I am stilling my mind and becoming silent.

D: I am glad you received the love of the children back at school this week. It was a very important turning point in your decision.

M: Yes and I'm having difficulty releasing it, joyful and stressful as it was.

D: Your function will always be in one way or another a teacher. In time you will advance from there, and find your skills developed.

M: That was my decision, which might have been too soon. I feel in one way, as though I was ready to advance, and in another, the longing to remain simple and joyful in the presence of the children.

D: There is still time for further studies and we can work on that as we progress.

D: Today, I would like to speak to you and to all reading this material about the body.

The body is an instrument of the soul. It is important to keep it in harmony lest it become out of balance and sick. This many of you do with overwork. There are energies and colors vibrating around the body at all times. These are there to keep you well and balanced. When you feel out of balance, you have the resources to come into contact with those watching over you. Your guides, angels and others who can in an instant, straighten out the situation. This is done with energy. Both yours and ours, so that harmony can again prevail.

Take a deep breath in. Feel us and our love around you. Release and repeat again. Become totally still with your thoughts. Release the emotions on all levels. Release and let go.

Lay down or sit. Feel the energy of the lower chakra, the one at the base of the spine. Allow it to move up to the next chakra, the sexual chakra, below your belly button. As this energy moves through you let each chakra cleanse the next.

M: Diana, there is a joyful sensation of energy moving.

D: Continue and go to the next chakra, the solar plexus. Take another deep and relaxing breath.

Let the energy continue to move through you as you give way to this process. The solar plexus is directly beneath your rib cage. Continue to deeply breath.

Now go to the heart chakra. This is the energy of love, balance and total wellbeing.

Feel all the energy raise up through your energy field. Let your heart shine with love. You may direct this at anyone who may need this upliftment at this time. Open your heart to others, don't close it off. It is the door to love, to being connected to everyone on the planet. This is the chakra that most needs opening for mankind to progress. For without love, we are as nothing, as it says in your scripture.

M: Diana, I want to thank you again for your healing touch.

D: My pleasure as always. It was a little more intense today due to the stress you were carrying.

D: The next chakra is that of the throat, or will. When you experience a sore throat you may be experiencing a conflict in your will. Your word goes forth from here. There is another chakra, which I haven't mentioned yet, it is slightly above the heart, near the thymus. This is important to the heart connection of mankind. It is not just a thymus, but part of a vibration of loving communication that will enable you to be more in touch with one another and the planet.

Let the energy continue up through the thymus and the throat. Continue to deeply breath.

D: The next chakra is the third eye. This is the chakra of the masters. These masters are sending out powerful thought energy to the earth grid as well as those with whom they are in touch. They use this gift with carefulness and discretion. Each master of mind can direct his or her total power in the earth's grid from this chakra. This determines the destiny of this person, and it is a seat of communication with other masters. It is the stuff where dreams are made!

D: The final chakra is the one on top of your head. The crown that all of you are wearing, to which I have referred before. This is the chakra of glory, healing and release. From this font you are healed, and also in touch with spirits, guides, angels and saints. When you feel elated, or when you speak, and you need help from above, this is the crowning energy we send you. You feel it as a special feeling of power, glory majesty. It is the very God head of your being. That is why your children delight in wearing crowns. Because they know they are so special.

1.Diana, Her Royal Radiance, watercolor by Marcia McMahon, © 2001.

Diana wears the Spencer crown here, as she attended a state dinner in her early career. To view this painting in color, go to: dianaspeakstotheworld.com

This painting is available in signed prints, go to the website to order.

The Eve of Diana's Anniversary, August 31st, 2001

Tonight I wish to speak with you about life and death, and the upward spiral that we are all on. It does not start with birth, and it does not end with death. You and I and all are all Immortal beings, emanating out from the God-head our truest source. I have described my so called death in other channeled writings, and from this perspective now, the circumstances of my death, as unfortunate as they seemed, were in divine timing with universe and cosmic occurrences. I am as loving, happy and contented in my spiritual dimension as I was when I lived as Diana on Earth. I am equally delighted to be present amongst you as I manifest through my channels. So, you see, I am Diana, Queen of Hearts, still! One might say that with channels in particular, I have had more than one lifetime!

From this unique vantage point, I can express through my channels and experience the life force once more, in all its glory and radiance. Therefore, in losing my physical form, I have taken on other forms. Though I am by no means the occupant of my channel's bodies, nor do I have permission to be. In my spiritual form, I feel very much the same Diana. Only, I can extend my thoughts to special situations in which I am needed and be there in spirit and in truth.

It is the will of our Heavenly Father Mother that we experience as much joy in the physical form as possible. The expression of life is utmost. We are to be the creative expressive dimension of God in whatever media we wish: painting, poetry, speaking, raising a family, writing, or just playful activity. We are the makers of our destiny, and the Earth is our playground. When one can look at life from this perspective, one is close to understanding the meaning of taking on a body. One takes on a body to experience and to express in physical form the truth within that one knows as one progresses up the spiral to God. At some point in the process, one expresses more love and more joy and then suddenly, one falls into the hands of God. This is then the homeward path to God, wherein the spiral meets itself, and one finds God, shall we say, in the mirror. The spiral descends back upon itself, and then descends into greater physical matter, and the process begins again.

As with an Ascended Master, there is no need to descend again into physical manifestation. One might think of us as angels in the truest sense. We have no real need to reincarnate. At the same time, we might enjoy another round of manifestation. We make no decisions lightly, and always our spiritual guides are there to advise us. As for my decision, I have no comment yet on that. I am an extremely happy expression through my channels and the messages I am able to convey for humanity at this time. It is a true pleasure for me to experience the dimension I reside in and to convey so much through my channels.

I wish to say here that my only regret is not being in physical form for my sons, William and Harry. I wish to be present with them in form, to caress them and hold them close. In time, it will be understood by them, if not already that I am not dead, but have merely transformed, or changed form in order to better serve the needs of humanity at this time. **The pain of my transition both physical and emotional was intense, but I am fully aware of the reasons why this was to be. A sting of regret and longing sometimes runs through me, but my boys know this in their hearts. In time, they**

will serve the human race and help to usher in the new era of hope for humanity.

Therefore, Darlings, just know how much I love you still!

I wish to thank all of you for the flowers you have laid at the Palace, and want you to know how much I love each one of you.

I am forever yours, Diana,
England's Rose.

I. An example of a tribute poster for Diana, here her dates (1961-1997) which says, Diana, the Peoples' Princess.
© photo, 2001, Marcia McMahon

II. Other views of the sea of flowers laid out for Diana, the Queen of Hearts at Kensington Palace.

III. A look of shock and grief betrayed on my bother Jim's face the day of Diana's funeral. My parents and Jim and another friend, Jim Wilson, were all at Diana's funeral by coincidence, and had airline tickets months in advance of her tragic day. They arrived an hour or two after the ceremony at Westminster Abbey. It was obviously a very moving experience for them, as it was for the millions who either attended or watched from their TV.

IV. Princess Diana-England's Rose with a candle burning, a memorial set up somewhere in London (I assume perhaps a museum) the day of her funeral. (Note: the picture of Diana, this was used in one of my paintings, see Diana Among the Cosmos) To view paintings in color, go to:

www.angelfire.com/mb2/diana_speaks/gallery_index.html/ **Diana Gallery One**, Paintings are available for a small fee, and they are signed prints.

V.. Here is a beautiful poster tribute to Diana, Princess of Wales, pictured here in her work with Bosnia. The hearts and flowers express the sentiments that Diana said were so true about so many of the floral tributes, that "the sentiments were true to heart" as she worded it in her Anniversary Message.

VI. Here is another poster/floral tribute to the couple, Diana and Dodi, apparently in French. Here we get a look at Dodi Fayed, who was quite handsome. Here the poster implies again an everlasting love.

VII. A view of the gates of Kensington Palace with roses and flowers the day of Diana's Funeral.

A beautifully arrayed spray of bouquets for Diana on the streets near Kensington Palace on that sad day for London and the world. © 2001, M. McMahon.

PREVIOUS PAGE

IX Here are the Harrod's department store tributes to both Diana, Princess of Wales and Dodi Fayad. I found these quite touching, since the many channeled messages from Diana refer to Dodi, who is with her. Many of the tributes touch the same note of everlasting love. Diana has quoted Dodi and on rare occasions his voice is heard in the channeled messages. Dodi is steadfast in his messages from the afterlife, admonishing his people, Muslims, to lead a good life and not give into the rhetoric or action of terror. Diana has referred to their love as an "eternal flame"

Diana: Mother Essence for the Children of Earth September 1, 2001

I wish to comment on the television production that you watched just now. (CNN Special on Diana, Princess of Wales) To again say thank you to my many viewers who knew me in life — as Diana, I am so overwhelmed and touched by your love. I had no idea I was loved so greatly! Know that you are also loved greatly by the Creator and by me, Diana, the People's Princess.

For each rose and each gift of love and remembrance is seen by me, and I watch over you with love. With each passing anniversary, I am still awed and amazed at all your love everywhere. If I could but materialize and show you myself again, just to return your love, I would. This message through my channel says it well, but not all of the love I have for you. I am a radiating center of love for the world now. Just call on my name and I'll be there for you to assist you in whatever trouble you might find.

Diana, is there anything else for William or Harry at this time? Well, essentially the message of my total loving presence with them at all times as they progress. They have an interesting role to play and will respond to my mothering role as was laid out for them from the beginning in the original plan. Take comfort my Darlings in my strength and my presence watching over you! I love you both greatly!

My charitable work with the children was so important to me. Because I loved both my boys so greatly and because I was a mother, going into those situations in Africa with AIDS was particularly painful to see. I was happy to lend a gentle hand of comfort on a dying child's hand, or to feed a hungry child. To see children in this condition was horrifying to me, even though I played the "role" of humanitarian. I love and adore children, and this was something that I both enjoyed touching those suffering, while at the same time, I felt it an unnecessary evil that there should be such an epidemic of AIDS, or hunger or famine. Children, all children, deserve the very best of our attentions. We bring them into this world, and we should do all we can to provide them the necessary food, shelter, clothing and protection from illness.

While most of the parents of the current world cannot afford to give children the very fundamental requirements of living well, we must globally and as a society move quickly to resolve that situation. A proper diet rich in enough protein, decent clothing, and a place of shelter are all that is necessary for the decent upbringing of children. Most importantly, your love is needed. You must make children your number one priority in this next millennium if the current world order is to evolve at all. This means all of you. I wish to thank those responsible for the handling of the funds set up in my name for the wonderful work they've been doing to relieve the plight of suffering everywhere, and in particular, those who continue my work with land mines and the most endangered children of all: those still suffering of AIDS in Africa. It is important that this work in my name continue, and that massive education of the spread of AIDS and of those less fortunate by my teachers now be stepped up! I want all who speak in my name and those who read my channeled books as well, to know how much love I have for the children of Earth at this time.

Not only am I requesting that the AIDS work continue but that the education of people in those countries by my teachers commence and then continue until such time those less fortunate can become independent of the given help. This is of the utmost. In the new era, education is the key to success in social, political and the new world order as it unfolds. So that the "have" nations can continue the charitable work, until the "have not" nations cease to exist. Much can be done on the internet by consumers particularly in the developed nations. Simply refuse to buy products manufactured by sweatshop labor, or child labor. That is but one example, there are many ways to politically assert one's pressure. Beware of bureaucrats who would simply continue the social injustice. Each one must insist on credibility of the various social agencies (charities) who are operating in the various countries. The children of Africa need your prayers and your money. Those of you still sitting in front of the television watching this tragedy go by must muster your conscience to the rescue. Africa needs your help, and will for some time. To those who can adopt orphaned children, please hear these children's cry for help. To those who have extra funds on hand, please give to my fund or the Red Cross. God bless you in advance of your desire to help in this way.

In closing then, the setting up of educational centers for those struggling with daily living skills, whatever they may be, is part of the entire reeducation program. I will appeal to those directors on the board of my fund to see that they understand the urgency of education of children and the parents, with setting up of after school programs or hunger centers so that there is not just a hand out, but a social system set up to help. I am asking this be done with my fund, the Diana, Princess of Wales Memorial Fund, at this time, and making no strings attached to the bargain. I thank you for your time in reading this my plea for the children of the world! I am the heartbeat of the Mother Essence for the Children of the Earth,

Diana.

9. Diana, Mother Comfort, watercolor, Marcia McMahon, © 2002 Diana, Mother Comfort, watercolor by Marcia McMahon © 2002 This was taken during Diana's visit to Chicago in 1996, where her obvious compassion overwhelms her. She hugs a very sick child here as she receives a bouquet of flowers from her. She was such a lovely Princess who cared for the suffering. To view this lovely watercolor go to www.angelfire.com/mb2/diana_speaks/gallery_index.html/ then to the Diana Gallery II.

The Potential Catastrophe September 8, 2001

M: Rereading your profound words on children, Diana, I am moved to do something very soon, contribute in some way beyond what I would normally.

D: That's very good. Now, I would like to go on with my message for today. Today's message involves the New Millennium, and the redirection of mankind's will to highest good for all.

As your reading suggests, I am part of the Holy Grail movement or enlightenment as Queen of Hearts. I am both Diana, the former Princess, and the archetype mother earth goddess, ready to assist all of you in ushering in the New Era that your hearts are longing for!

At this precarious juncture, the Earth and its inhabitants are threatened by many potential environmental dangers. Those in coastal areas are particularly endangered, due to the fact, as your scientists have already pointed out, of your polar ice caps melting. This in turn will cause the oceans to rise, drastically affecting life as we know it on Earth. Whilst much can be done to prevent massive loss of life, those in coastal areas need to pay particular attention to weather patterns and to moving from areas of low tidal inundation. This is in no way an exaggeration: all will be affected.

You, as the emerging new human species on the planet have collectively created this potential catastrophe and can, with enough collective consciousness detonate the possible time bomb well in advance of this disaster. But you must collectively change your world view and consciousness so that this occurrence will not manifest. It will commence at the beginning as tropical storms, too numerous to count, and build up to very fast raging storms, out of control with massive waves toppling buildings and structures around coastal areas. In essence it will speed up with great momentum, faster than your scientists predicted and find many of you unaware and unprepared. That is why, from my standpoint I have been permitted to speak to those of you who will listen to these predictions about the weather patterns.

While on the one hand, these tendencies exist as very real phenomenon, on the other hand, the human species has to look to scientists to tell them what we as beings of light are telling those who will listen with an open heart. You will be able to survive this kind of change only if you will look within, to the God self. If you will begin to see one another as brothers and sisters and assist in those areas where disaster hits the hardest, those lessons of love will uplift the consciousness of the entire planet.

M: Forgive my interruption Diana, but we had a massive storm predicted today, and I sat out in my garden watching butterflies. In my mind I only thought it was a glorious sunny day, and the storm never manifested. Is it possible to avert the bigger storm that is predicted in so many New Age writings by using one's thought energy?

D: Well, that is it precisely! You yourself didn't want another thunderstorm and continued to focus on the outside beauty, keeping it in consciousness. If enough of you will do just that much pain and suffering can be averted. But not all pain and suffering. Earth has changed, and her ozone layer is fast being depleted. Much environmental damage has been done, some irreversible.

Yet, I come to give all a message of hope who will open their ears. Your race is destined for glory! And many on this side maintain that the hoped for 1,000 years of peace will quickly ensue after a brief period of catastrophe ensues, assuring the continuation of life on Earth as we know it.

M: Diana, is there anything we can do besides elevate our consciousness? What are your suggestions for practical living? Save seeds, save tropical plants for reintegration into the areas where inundation has receded?

D: At this juncture there is much that can be done. If you live in a coastal area, reevaluate your real needs to be there. If you live inland, begin by making sure you have access to water purification.

Saving seeds is fine, as are other measures for emergency use, such as canned food and alternate sources of energy use. Do all you can for the environment right now. Farmers need to use organic methods of farming before all the topsoil is gone. Pesticides are a definite hazard to everyone's health, affecting even your genetic structures.

Try to eat an organic diet, avoiding meats as much as possible. Continue to live in love for one another as much as possible. The emotions of hate are as poisonous to the system as are the toxic chemicals in your dumping grounds.

Earth was once a true paradise. It will be up to the next generation of children being born now to make it that way again, starting one by one as you did before descending from the Ark with your seeds, your goats and cattle. I speak in metaphors but the analogy is the same. There will unfortunately be massive inundation with coastal waters, but you as a race can take refuge now.

M: Then, there is to be a flood of sorts?

D: I am just giving the predictions, there are no assurances in prophecy. The best prophets are those whose predictions never come true. I would like to assure my readers here that those who care about the earth, about others and are nurturing beings will likely survive to continue the species. The DNA is programed this way, for the new wave of human species will have compassion in its genes, as rightly it should be, thereby giving the new human a gene for compassion! This then will ensue a generation of compassionate humans who will not be able to harm themselves, thereby helping to redirect the former energies of so many misguided humans to do harm to others.

We here in spirit will be assisting those human beings who will be instrumental in the new leadership once the time of catastrophe has subsided.

M: Whew, what an incredible prediction! It matches those of the other prophets about our Earth changes. Some even say that we can avert this with pure consciousness alone.

D: That is true. There would need to be enough of you in agreement on this principle. As it still stands now, there are many in industrialized nations who make wealth a form of aggrandizement at the expense of the rain forest, the child laborer, the impoverished nations whose natural resources are being raped from the ground up. Unless this exploitation stops, the likelihood is great for world weather disaster. Your polar ice caps are melting, this your scientists already confirm.

M: I see, we have a situation already in process. Is it true about the San Andreas fault line, and the earthquake of 1990 in California? Was Jesus there trying to avert the ripple effect of that earthquake?

D: Jesus the Christ or Sananda as we know him was there, yes. As to whether it was to be the disaster that was to bring down the world as we know it, that I am not able to speak on.

Sananda is here with me in my healing efforts, even as we worked with you. He is always an intercessor for the human condition.

M: Forgive my ignorance on this but why do you call him Sananda? It seems very Eastern and mystical but we always refer to him as Jesus Christ. Is that not correct?

D: Sananda is his proper name. Just as you have a first and last name, so does he! Jesus the Christ is more accurate, for he was the manifestation of Christ energy and power when he lived as Jesus the Christ. Before he was known as Sananda, therefore his primary title still holds.

M: I am humbled and still a little confused but I really don't need to know everything just yet.

It seems knowing what you told me (about weather patterns) is a little mind boggling and the need to know diminishes my sense to continue needing to know!

D: That is as it should be for now.

M: Is there anything else at this juncture?

D: We will continue a little later. You wish to walk in your beautiful sunny garden. Enjoy the beauty of the day!

SEPTEMBER 11, 2001 World Trade Centers Collapse after terrorists hijacked planes and strike them, and the Pentagon is also struck by a plane and part of it collapses. Then another plane, apparently hijacked, crashes in rural Pennsylvania.

Diana's Wisdom on the September 11th Attacks September 15, 2001

M: Diana, I am asking your guidance on the situation now facing us as humans, especially in light of the September 11, 2001 tragic loss of life in New York (World Trade Center Twin Towers) and Washington (the Pentagon).

D: All of us watched in horror the events of the past week. We on the spirit side are with those grieving for lost loved ones and for those seriously injured. All on this side send love and special support at this critical time.

M: I assumed Diana, that you were very busy greeting those passing over from the World Trade Centers, the airplanes and the Pentagon.

D: Yes, it is true. My job now entails comfort and rest for the newly departed souls. Many are totally in shock and horror here, now as we speak. Going through death with just a moments notice is very difficult. We are here to help all, and continuing our help for the living I will shortly comment on the difficult times ahead for all the world.

At this important and sad juncture in the history of the world, all humans have a decision to make. Will they choose more hatred and war or will they choose tolerance and peace? It appears that your very world is teetering on collapse from a possible WWIII. While mass murder is in no way a tolerable act, the next step, that of attacking other nations assumed responsible may result in an inevitable World

War III. In a fury of retaliation and possible need to strike back, the Western Allies may find themselves in an unprecedented dilemma. What to do with those responsible for the horrible attack of the World Trade Center and the Pentagon, and what to do with the situation.

I will caution you again: Think twice before you strike back! Terror will reign if this action is taken, with many more innocent lives at stake. Not just those Arab nations, but all of the middle eastern nations and many allies of Arab countries will find themselves due to trade or proximity about to side. The American President is also a possible target during his entire presidency. If the terrorists didn't succeed last week, they believe they will succeed again and again. If his presidency is terminated, much chaos will reign due to the last elections, thereby creating a power vacuum, which is just what the "enemy" wants. Whilst I am here in the seventh heaven, you on Earth must still decide what role you as emerging humanity want for your world. St. Francis said it so well in the 13th century.

Make me an instrument of your peace Where there is hatred let me sow love Where there is injury, let me sow pardon Where there is friction, let me sow union Where there doubt, let me sow faith.

Where there is despair, let me sow hope. Where there is darkness, let me sow light, Where there is sorrow, let me sow joy.

Oh, Divine Master, let me not so much seek to be comforted as to comfort.

To be understood as to understand, to be loved as to love,

For it is in dying that we are born to eternal life.

It may seem incomprehensible to choose peace in such a world that has been shattered. I commend you all for the bravery and brotherly love you have shown in New York and Washington. If you can do that for yourselves then do it for those you don't understand. Those souls living in the Arab nations, subject to regimes whose political and religious jargon you don't understand. Understand that many in those countries are kept in ignorance due to lack of education, especially the women and children. Give those nations a chance to produce the terrorists on their own, and then to begin to work towards governmental policies of tolerance of religious differences. It was no "accident" that Dodi and I "left" at our mutual time. **The World needed to see a Muslim, a Christian and a Catholic (Mother Teresa) pass into spirit at the same time, thereby creating a kind of equality.**

All must face death, and religion is for the edification of the spirit, not the destruction of it by mutual hatreds. Please understand that God does not will destruction of this kind for his children. His will is always life and peace, and in that same line of thought, so should your united wills be: that of life and peace at this critical juncture. I wish to add that peace is still an option, and to ask all to pray for a way to see it through at this critical time. My loving help and presence is always available. Peace be with you, all my loving comfort,

Diana.

Diana: A Consolation in a Troubled Time Diana's Words on the World Trade Center and Pentagon September 22, 2001

M: Diana, I just want to thank you for your presence today at the healing session.

D: You are most welcome. You see that Jan sees my presence coming to you in a kind arc. I have spoken of this before. It is the sphere wherein the seventh heaven folds back upon itself, and that is what is quite unique about me now. Your worries that I am detained helping others whilst I am helping you are not quite so. My etheric essence can be anywhere and quite powerful too.

So I am really constantly available to everyone who might need me.

M: That is quite amazing. I would say that being in the third dimension is a little limiting considering the possibilities!

D: Yes and no. There is nothing quite like it, being in a body form!

Diana's Words on the World Trade Center

I now want to cover the topic of world peace and world war. The situation that has arisen out of the terrorist attack on the World Trade Center and the Pentagon, has now become quite serious.

While the armies of the world unite in alliances, be aware that more terror is being planned.

I urge you all to take cover, especially in the United States. Avoid air travel for a time more. Worry about economic recovery later. If the Arab nations feel threatened with bombs and air strikes, they may retaliate with more of the same that was the absolute horror of the World Trade Center. Sadly, the world has seen nothing like this perpetrated upon US soil. It is reminiscent of the WWII theater where so much life was lost and buildings were bombed. Our British people can testify to the horror of the blitz and nightly air raids.

Americans and Britons alike can reflect upon past alliances and secure their future now with strong alliances and at the same time, take time to understand the position of the lesser Arab nations, such as Afghanistan and Uzbekistan. I am speaking now for all to come to peace instead of arms.

While ample time was given to allow for the release of the terrorist Osama Bin Laden, the country of Afghanistan realized that outright civil war would be perpetrated upon them by the terrorist for giving him up. In essence, they had no real power to release him to US authorities for trial.

While he in fact is the perpetrator of these crimes against humanity, there are many others operational in other Arab and allies of Arab nations. **Dodi wishes to say to his people (of Egypt) and those of moderate Arab countries of the world that they should hold fast to peace and not move to the same tactics and the same rhetoric. He is saying that Allah is the God of all people, not just Muslim nations. He is saying that the Koran does not sanction terror, and all who participate in terror blaspheme the Holy One, Allah.** He further wishes to warn those groups in Egypt that any terror perpetrated upon the US would only contribute to the worsening of the world situation, and would not serve God, therefore it would not be a holy war in any sense of the word.

"Palestine, be warned!" he says, "violence at this time will further hurt your chances of securing a homeland in the Middle east. It would turn the US totally against you and bring down your leader as well!"

While I have concentrated my steadfast effort in the message on the dynamics of World political issues at this time, I am fully aware and have seen in time, the possible world that you all can build for one another. This is a world where human cooperation and understanding are mandated by all civilized governments. Where religion is a means of edification of the spirit and not an excuse for bloodshed and hatred. Don't be duped by those in control into thinking that the world needs war at this time. It is part of the military industrial complex which feeds upon the collective fear of the planet. It could not literally exist if fear were eliminated by those thinking individuals who so choose to renounce its chains upon their minds. John Lennon put it so well in the song Revolution.

"You say you want a revolution, well, we all want to change the world. When you go talking about minds that hate, you ain't gonna make it with anyone anyway. You know it's gonna be, all right, you know it's gonna be all right." Well, in time my dear friends, it will. You each must choose the collective destiny of the planet in all you do. My love, light and prayers for the world are with you all, **I am forever your consolation in a troubled time,**

Diana.

4. Diana in Egypt, watercolor, Marcia McMahon, ©

2001 Princess Diana always dressed to reflect respect for the customs of the country she visited. Here, she is in Egypt, wearing a veil and viewing the sky, or perhaps the spire to a Minaret. She always got along well in Arab countries and was well loved by those countries and their leaders. Diana is able to address Arab issues, having met many of the current leaders of the Arab world.There are many pictures of her visiting Saudi Arabia, visiting the Crown Prince. Watercolor titled, Diana in Egypt by Marcia McMahon, © 2001, all rights reserved. To view Diana in Egypt in color, go to:

www.angelfire.com/mb2/diana_speaks/gallery_index.html(then go to Diana Gallery One)

All Americans Take Cover! September 28, 2001

M: M: Diana, I am wondering what we can do to help in any way with the situation in the world?

D: Finding peace within oneself is the answer to almost every dilemma: political, social, or global.

M: As the song goes, "Let there be peace on earth and let it begin with me!"*[2]

D: Yes, that is so true. Whilst we all must search for peace within ourselves through whatever means available, such as meditation, we are collectively as a planet preparing for war. This is the choice of your leaders serving the interests of the people. Again I warn you all to think again. The prospects of WWIII are looming large on the horizon. Is this kind of action what you want? Must thousands of innocent lives be given up to bombs and hatred? While there wasn't much chance for negotiation in Afghanistan, due to the situation there with internal conflict (which already exists), civil war would break out if the terrorist Osama Bin Laden were to be released to the US authorities. This is the reason why the US must pursue a path of continued surveillance and negotiation with moderate Arab nations who will help. To go in with the full force of an air raid will have an immediate and horrible effect in the United States. Again, I urge all Americans to take cover if the air raid occurs, more terror and more horror will be inflicted.

---

[2] Words and music by Sy Miller and Jill Jackson - 1955

M: Okay, Diana, I thank you for the warning. I want to know can you specify what type of cover we as Americans need at this time and what kind of terror would be perpetrated? I am frightened, and we all can use some of your wisdom here on what type of horror they might be planning.

D: In the same vein as the World Trade Center. More terror on the airplanes from hijackers. They also have biological and chemical weapons which would be used from the airplanes upon entire cities. Those in the largest cities would be most affected and would cause the greatest damage and loss of life. Large and important centers of trade and commerce would be their obvious targets. Incapacitating of the presidency and other important offices will also be their terrible agenda.

M: If the US uses a policy of moderation, surveillance and intelligence just to bring those perpetrators to justice, could that be enough to stop further loss of life and prevent the War?

D: This is a radical departure from the thinking of the Pentagon and those who in the past have succeeded in the last war, the so called Gulf War. Those same countries and individuals who felt they lost the most would be those to look out for and to be aware of terrorist activities, including the following countries: Afghanistan, Uzbekistan, Iraq, Iran, United Arab Emirates, (terror factions) Yemen, (terror factions) some terrorist hubs are located in Egypt, known to all of you as Jihad, and there are terrorist operations all throughout Western European countries. There is a unity under them which they feel is Islam, but it is pure rhetoric in the extreme. **In fact, Dodi says it is a perversion of the Islam that most devout Muslims practice. He wishes to say that the Jihad (organization) is a blaspheme upon Allah, the One True God. And those who participate in such practices of terror do not inherit eternal life, but find they see the horror and the murder which they have perpetrated when they reach the spirit world.** Those who do this inherit the terror they perpetrate. While there is no hell in spirit, this is the closest thing to hell as one could define it. He wishes again to warn his brethren not to buy into the extremist rhetoric that is becoming widespread throughout the Arab world.

M: Is there any hope in the scenario? Especially since this book was devoted to finding Heaven on Earth and peace for the world's children, as you originally conceived it?

D: Peace is always an option. Those who choose war upon others choose it upon themselves. There can be no other way. But in the interests of the Allied Nations, it is seen at this juncture as a necessary evil. I wish to clarify that it is seen as the only alternative to the evil known now as terrorism. Nations will rise against nation, as it says in your holy Bible. Your world is teetering upon collapse. It was my ardent hope[3] and dream for a world of peace, cooperation and understanding. Know all of you affected by this decision that you are greatly loved by your Creator and that all life is eternal, as is evidenced in this channeling.

---

[3] "Ardent hope" was referenced in reading Shadows of a Princess by P.Jephson, her personal secretary. These same words were penned in a letter to the Ambassador for Northern Ireland, when she expressed her "ardent hope" for peace in Northern Ireland, and Ireland. p. 336 It is noteworthy to mention that I read "Shadows" six months after this channeled message

I would ask that all pray for peace and a miracle for the world at this time. My heartfelt prayers are with those who stand for peace in a world torn asunder by violence at this time. I keep you all in my heart at this critical juncture. I am the heartbeat of peace and consolation for all of you who call on me. My eternal love,

Diana

On Love and Leaving the Body October 3, 2001

M: Diana, here I am today come to greet you, meet you on the page. It is all I can do to simply be here to hear your voice. I am feeling a little lonely, depressed or sad. It is being without family that makes me feel this way, and the fact that they don't understand me, or our communications.

D: Yes, we all have sadness, pain and loneliness. You are never alone, for the angels and guides are with you, and were with you on the path today as you were painting, or trying to. You fell, dumped your water out, and then you knew it was time to return home, to finish the lovely portrait you're doing of me, my remembrance as Diana. I want you to know that you are indeed loved and appreciated not just by those of us in spirit who look on, but admired greatly by the fortunate who know you! **You surely must have sensed this when you left your teaching position recently, the magnitude of the children's love for you!**

M: Oh, yes, and I felt as though I was in a magnetic pull with their love and admiration. That I was very much at home there, and then suddenly I had to depart.

D: Well said, and I felt much the same way when I left the Earth plane. It was as though the love wave was so intense and magnetic that I hesitated to leave my body, just to linger in the love for a moment more; but then it was gone, and I moved on to greater realms of love! Love is the reason we are all here in the first place. It is always saddening to have to leave, and then the love seems less but it isn't. It just transmutes to another level, plane or circumstance.

Diana's Plea for Prayer and Peace October 6, 2001

D: I wish to return to world affairs for a time, and to further remind our readers that it is time to continue to pray for world peace. Even your leaders are beginning to welcome this idea.

M: Diana, I am amazed that the State Department knows what you know. Specifically you told me that if the air raids were to begin over Afghanistan, then more terror would reign on the United States. Now, I see on the news that the State Department put out the same warning. They said that if air attacks on Afghanistan were to begin, there is a 100% chance of another outright terrorist attack on another building or city.

D: Yes, my information is entirely correct and why shouldn't it be? All knowledge is available here, about events past, present and future. What isn't known even here in eternity is what the choices will be in the future. Every choice and outcome can be viewed as though on a CD rom, but the choices are still those of humanity to make. It is my job to insure the future of the race by sending my messengers of light to reach out as a beacon in the darkness of the mass consciousness to create and recreate the kind of world all of you wish to create. To remind all that they are continuously creating their world by every thought, word and deed. And so it is that all of you are co-creators with the One true Creator God! You must make your collective destiny. And of course we serve to guide you all, gently influencing those who have power of choice for the many.

I am close to Prime Minister Tony Blair, as he and I held a friendship before my passing. It was then it was decided privately that I should become an "Ambassador" for Britain, but now of course, for peace. He is an excellent man of integrity and superb leadership for England. I also watch over your President and his advisors and know the intentions of his heart are for good, though his rhetoric may sound a little antiquated for the New Age which is to dawn.

I would like to thank everyone for their heartfelt prayers at this time. Christians, Muslims and Jews can learn to pray and work together to appreciate differences without resorting to crimes of hatred and bloodshed over religious differences. **It says in your Holy Bible in the words of your beloved teacher Jeshua, to love one's enemies and pray for those who persecute you. In the minds of so many now, we realize this humbling truth that our Way Shower has pointed out. In the silence of the mind without prejudice, we are One in truth and stand beside our Creator together side by side.**

Love of one's enemies is the answer to the dilemma now facing all of you: Christian, Muslim or Jew. Whether you live in Israel, in Iraq or Iran, everyone the world over must continue to pray for enemies. In this, I ask all of you no matter your religious persuasion. So much of the conflict is still over religious righteousness, which in spirit, is pure rhetoric. It (religious righteousness) is the dominance of one human over another, and God does not discriminate. All meet the Creator at the gate of death, and all are regarded equal here; no matter what religious practice you adhered to on Earth.

I commend all of you for your continued effort in prayer and ask that it continue, so that the world will be transformed one by one, within each one's heart, that peace will reign supreme in the heart.

For those who are preparing instead for war, I ask again, think twice for what you perpetrate upon another you perpetrate upon yourselves. There is no justification for war upon the helpless Afghan people, or for more terror on the United States! Your leaders are pursuing a middle ground in seeking the terrorists, and this is highly commendable, for in time they will be caught and their terrible deeds and agendas brought to light for all the world to see. It is possible to choose an alternate agenda, that of the middle ground of peace thereby saving yourselves the horror and havoc of a possible WWIII. All leaders listening to my messages need to understand the gravity of the situation, as it is extremely serious. Think of your children, and your children's children! They deserve to be offered a life, not a contaminated planet of nuclear disaster or chemical weapons, but a beautiful Earth free and safe for human habitation. **Your God and his angels bow gently to you and simply ask that you do justly with one another, love God and your Earth to save a future for your children's children.**

I am an Ambassador for Peace in the World and a consolation in a troubled time,

Diana.

To Christians, Muslims and Jews October 13, 2001

M: Diana, I'm here for you.

D: Good, and thank you for your choice to be with me, as our readers are also with me in spirit now as I speak.

M: Is there any topic you with to cover today?

D: Well, to begin with, your web site is beautiful and I would like to thank Maria for her efforts in putting it together so beautifully. My messages will in time be read by just those people who need to read them, and showcasing them in a fitting package will help my cause on Earth, which of course is Peace.

M: Diana, you couldn't have said it better, the web site is a fitting tribute to your words and something lovely for the world to see, to think about at this time.

I am wondering how can we know if these messages are really coming from you? Forgive me any rudeness in the question but I am getting this response when I mention your channeling to some.

D: Truth stands on its own merit, its own accord. The only way to verify the message is to let it resound within your soul, and if it's true, it will resound accordingly. I work through other channels and each one is a filter through which my words resonate. Some are more accurate than others, and all have human faults. In all fairness to the question, I can verify the truth of this channel, you.

But the reader must also make up their own mind, and this is so true in any endeavor, in anything one reads. Put aside judgments and prejudice as you read my material so that my voice can be heard around the world and within your own heart.

I wish to commend the efforts of so many working on worthy causes now that the war has broken out. The emphasis on the humanitarian efforts in Afghanistan with regard to the food shortages is a very important cause which will show the world and the Afghan people that the American people care about them, and understand the oppression of the Taliban government there.

Again I wish to say to all Americans, take cover, be careful and watchful in the days ahead! There is still terror being planned, and I commend the United States for taking the necessary precautions to avoid another disaster like the World Trade Center. It is my ardent hope for a peaceful resolution to the situation now unfolding in the world. Again I ask all Christians, Muslims and Jews to pray for peace and understanding as I did in my last message. To ask all again to forgive their enemies and to pray for those who persecute you, (as Jesus the Christ recommended we do.) This is indeed the solution to misunderstandings and religious righteousness which is at the heart of the conflict we are now in.

Please understand that God does not will suffering upon anyone. That it is his will for all his people everywhere for peace and justice without vengeance. That one point alone suffices to understand that God could not conceive of a holy war, or vengeance of any kind. To wage

war in his name is to misunderstand the Creator, whose will is peace for all peoples and all nations.

There is a way of living in the world that makes peace possible and that is forgiveness. If one wishes to find any lasting peace, forgiveness of one's enemies is the very beginning at least. Take time out of your daily lives to pray for peace and to forgive. I am with all of you who call on me, in spirit and in truth, I am your consolation in a troubled time,

Diana

Diana: Further Warning; Dodi: Message to Muslims October 20, 2001

M: Diana, I heard your call, so here I am on the page. Is there any pressing issue you wish to speak about today?

D: Thank you for being in spirit with me now, as many readers are also with me in spirit as I speak.

I would like you to know that your healing is complete, even though you had some residual anxiety about the treatment you received from Jan and then from me, in spirit.

M: Thank you for clarification on that point, for I was uneasy that the treatment didn't take.

D: And I knew you were. We worked round the clock that evening on your heart, so that residual chords of energy were being pulled out of your body and auric field.

M: Diana, you are such a personnel blessing in my life, and to the world from your unique vantage point, and I want to say how much I love you, in spirit!

D: Thank you and you are loved by me and so many here for who you are and for the work you are doing for everyone to bring my voice to just those persons who need to hear it!

I wish to return to world affairs for a time, until the situation calms down a bit, and comes to a successful resolution. My beloved sister in truth, I wish now to return for a time to the situation at hand, which is still quite serious.

While alliances are being formed throughout the Arab world, most underground, there is still terror being planned.

M: Thank you again for the warning, Diana. Is there any thing we should be aware of or plan for?

D: Again, I caution you about the airplanes, for that is where they wish to strike. It would be wise to implement plans of actions for each airline, so that they have adequate defenses in the cockpit for the pilot, be it arms or be it a gas or stun gun. And I ask that the stewardesses and stewards be trained and possibly armed. This way, the flying can resume safely without interruption to the US and world economy!

M: Whew! Diana, that is a brilliant suggestion and I think they are working on stun guns, I saw that on the news. About using guns, I am a bit surprised at that idea coming from the Princess we know to be peace and love?

D: I am all peace and love, but am practical too! I would never suggest harm to another. A gun to defend oneself against the terrorist attack will prevent them from sabotage, from further hijacking.

M: This is an important idea. While the gun might never need to be used, it would adequately protect the pilot. What about a bar to protect them from entering the cockpit as well?

D: All such defenses are necessary at this point I am afraid, you see many Muslims feel there is a unity among them known as Islam, but as I said before, it is pure rhetoric in the extreme.

Dodi wishes to say to his people again be warned. **"Further terror will only hurt your cause for a homeland for Palestine! This week's terror perpetrated by Hamas will have worldwide repercussions, for Israel will not tolerate that level of hatred. He wishes to say that Muslims everywhere should unite in peace and love and try to show the world the real meaning of the religion that Muhammad intended, not the hatred and evil that the extremist terrorists are propagating.**

To do further harm will only make a mockery of the beautiful religion he knows as Islam. Purity and righteousness living in the bands of love of one another, including enemies, is the true religion he practiced. Devout Muslims unite in peace, love and unity with those of the faith and those who are not Muslims, he says, only in this way will we repair the tarnished reputation in the eyes of the world right now. As for the extremists (terrorists), they are a perversion of the true Islam. Don't listen to them and don't buy into their jargon."

M: Diana, I am so glad that Dodi is commenting on the events from the standpoint of a devout and good Muslim. It means so much to get a different take on the world view at the moment, especially those of us who are Christians, and westerners.

D: Dodi is playing a crucial role right now for the millions of readers I will shortly have in time on the web site and in the new book. If humanity can learn to be tolerant of religious differences even in these troubled times, then the world can be transformed to a beautiful world of love and peace for our children, and our children's children. **One heart and one heartbeat at a time, and the "world can be as one," in the words of the great lyric poet and musician, John Lennon, who is with me in spirit from time to time!**

M: You've quoted his message more than once Diana, and of course we all loved him and his message.

D: He was a prophet in his own time, and his words echo in the hearts and minds of many on earth, and throughout eternity as well. He influenced the magnetic grid surrounding the world, so powerful were his words and music. He was a transformer of the human race and so was I, in my life as Diana, Princess of Wales.

M: It sounds as though you were playing in a starring role instead of just living a life.

D: That is so, and rightly should it be thought of, although I had thoughts and emotions, my life as Diana was like super stardom, even in the darkest moments of personal tragedy, such as my divorce and death. People everywhere looked to my life, perhaps too much in the tabloids and missed the meaning of my life, which was to be an example amongst the people. For you are all capable of greatness and must learn to look within oneself for the inner Princess or Prince!

For now I wish to close with this thought that you are to look within your own heart, seek your own greatness and find something to do for humankind to show your love and goodness. I continue to watch over all of you and ask for continued prayer amongst the faithful in all religious persuasions so that the conflict will soon end. **I am with you all in spirit and in truth, and a consolation in a troubled time, all my love,**

Diana,

Princess of Love.

Afghan Politics and Issues and Her Words to Elton John October 27, 2001

M: Diana, here I am as well today ready to hear from you.

D: Thank you, I am pleased to be with you now in spirit. My pleasure always.

M: Mine, too. You always display the exquisite manors of your royalty, Diana.

D: Yes and the world needs manners right now.

M: I am sure mine are not what they should be either, we Americans are sometimes impatient and known to be rude.

D: I would like again to return to world affairs for a time. It seems as this time that the war is worsening, and still the bombings persist. Britain has called in special troops to fight the Taliban government.

M: Yes, Di, and I was glad to see that in a way. The alliance you spoke of weeks ago is still strong between Britain and America.

D: Yes, on the one hand our strong alliances are very good and serve as protection for both countries and the world. It is seen as the only means of dealing with the evil of the terrorists which is highly commendable.

M: Certainly the terrorists won't win this war.

D: Unlikely indeed for what they stand for is terror, even to their own people who are very frightened by the recent execution of the moderate leader, Haq.

M: Yes, I was upset by that. The fashion of the execution and the horror of it, the absolute barbarism involved. It was a statement of sheer barbarism.

D: Well spoken, though they felt it necessary to kill anyone not in their camp, that of the Taliban government. The situation that has arisen out of the continued bombing has left a wasteland for the Afghan people, and they are in danger of starving over the winter. I wonder now when enough will be enough for them, I am speaking only from a humanitarian point of view. I am asking that the bombing stop soon and that the terrorists be caught without all this suffering inflicted upon the Afghan people.

M: I don't blame you for your plea. I just don't have the personal power to make them do anything, much less change the course of world events.

D: But you see you are helping a very noble cause right here right now, just by listening to my voice and being a willing peace participant.

M: I am always honored to listen Diana. I'll deliver the message even though our thoughts may differ on fine points. I don't want the Afghan people to starve and neither does our government, the United States. They are dropping food and bombs both, and we can't be sure where these are going.

D: It is sad to observe the suffering there, and know that perhaps a middle ground could be obtained that of an offensive only on the Taliban, the terrorist Osama Bin Laden, and the regime. I urge all leaders listening to my message to continue in their efforts and to concentrate their efforts on the Taliban government, while offering humanitarian assistance to the helpless Afghan people. It will fare better in the eyes of the world if the U.S. stops engaging so many other Afghan cities and concentrates strictly on the mission at hand.

M: Is that all for today?

D: My message is concluding shortly. **I wish to say that you all are to be commended for your noble actions everywhere, for now is a time for those who wish to serve the human race to come forth and serve with kindness, gentleness and love. And to give generously from your hearts. I wish to thank those involved in helping everywhere, including my fund, The Diana, Princess of Wales Fund. I wish to personally thank Elton John for his marvelous concert last night, and again to say thank you for your tribute to me, "Candle in the Wind", and to all those who support my cause in the world at this time.** Give generously at this time to those without. I ask all everywhere to continue your ardent prayers for a peaceful resolution to this conflict. **I am forever England's Rose and a consolation in a troubled time.**

All my love, Diana.

Diana's Message November 2, 2001

M: Diana, I'm here as requested for you.

D: I'm glad you found a way. Things have been a bit hectic this day for you.

M: Yes, but I wonder what you have on your mind tonight?

D: I am thinking of your well being tonight.

M: Oh? I think I am well.

D: It might be best to rest a while and try the channeling tomorrow when you are fresh.

M: Okay. I just thought with all that discussion with Maria you might have to comment on our discussions.

D: In time my darling I will.

A Plea for the Helpless Afghan People November 3, 2001

M: Here I am Diana.

D: Yes, you're feeling much better rested. I can now comment on the days ahead.

Whilst there is much turmoil due to the bombings in Afghanistan, I wish to still make a plea that the bombing subdue. Many Afghans are now starving and helpless without shelter due to the intensive bombing of the Allied Forces there.

M: Yes, Di, I've seen it all over the news. It does seem relentless.

D: Relentless and horrific, both. Speaking from a purely humanitarian point of view, it seems senseless. It was my ardent hope that this mission would focus on intelligence and surveillance rather than mass bombing of the helpless Afghan people. I must comment on the Arab nations at this time. Some are now seeing the destruction and fearing it will be them next. Therefore the threat of a terrorist surprise attack is now very great. At the same time, the moderate Arab nations see Osama Bin Laden and his network of terrorists for what they are: **propagandists who are on mission impossible, from suicide to murder and no real platform to uphold their twisted ideals. This is as it should be: for they are about evil and lies even in the name of Islam.**

M: Diana, your message is very eloquent. I hope more people read your words on the web site, and in the new book.

D: In time, my darling friend, it will be so.

M: Is that your request for today?

D: That is all for now. I wish to say to those reading these messages that they are true. That my channel is listening very carefully to my voice as best she can. **She is a messenger of light for the world at this time, and those who are finding fault with her or my message should see the honesty and integrity of her message and mine, as we become one in this channeling. To prejudge her or my message is to miss the message entirely; for she is quite genuine and on the path of truth.**

I urge all to continue in prayer and unity so that in every way you will build up the human race right where you are. All listening to my messages need to pray continually at this point so that the world will not be ruined by this war. For your children and your children's children, think of them. I am a voice of love and consolation in a troubled time.

My love, Diana.

Warnings of Weapons of Mass Destruction November 10, 2001

M: Diana, I am here for you.

D: Thank you my darling.

M: Yes, is there anything you wish to speak on today?

D: The continued bombing of Afghanistan. I am wondering when enough will be enough.

M: Yes, I sympathize with those poor people having their homes bombed out.

D: It's quite devastated, really.

M: We don't see all that. We heard they took Mazarree-Shariff.

D: Yes, taking at what cost? The entire nation is a literal wasteland. I am afraid the US and Britain will have to clean up the mess, at a huge cost to their own economy.

M: Di, I am so thankful for your repeated warnings, and that no terrorists have succeeded yet at further harm.

D: Your State Department has done an excellent job in fending off much of the terror. I wish to say though that they are still planning terror, and are now investing in chemical weapons as well as nuclear weapons. That this threat needs to be taken seriously, because they won't hesitate to use it if they can get their hands on it. And they wish to blow up as many as they possibly can now.

M: Sounds like they are on a vengeance streak.

D: That is putting it mildly. And many Arab nations are with them in this plot. Many wish to do harm still to the US and allies.

M: Thanks again, Di, for the warnings. Do you think that the President did a good job in trying to commit moderate Arab nations to the task of terrorist expulsion?

D: He couldn't do it all, and did rightly to ask for the moderate Arab nations to join in the game. They have everything to gain and nothing to lose. But as I said previously, they are to be watched cautiously, for they harbor terrorists unwittingly.

M: Oh, I have heard that before!

D: Yes and many play the public role of monitor whilst they then make secret arrangements for the protection of Osama Bin Laden and his people. I am sorry to report that not all can be trusted.

M: That is troubling to know, Diana.

D: I would like to conclude todays' brief message with a thought on love. That you are all to be commended on the amount of love you show everywhere towards one another and towards your countries. That all are asked to continue to show brotherly love and compassion toward the less fortunate, and that all are asked to pray that this conflict doesn't break out into an outright world war.

If all could love enough, just for one day, the world would be transformed. And that there is no shortage of love, so while I send my love to each one of you, I ask you then to send yours on for the good of all.

All my love with you at this time, I am Diana,
England's Rose.

On Afghanistan and Terrorists Elsewhere November 17, 2001

M: I am here for you in silence today, Diana.

D: I am grateful to have a willing channel for the many who will hear my messages.

M: My pleasure as always, Diana.

D: Today the world issues are pressing in on us from everywhere. I wish to address the nations as they begin the task of peacekeeping for Afghanistan. It is known everywhere throughout the Arab world that many nations in the Arab world harbor terrorists. So while the war bombed out much of Afghanistan, it did not eradicate the threat of terror elsewhere in the world.

M: You mean that we haven't accomplished our goal of liberating Afghanistan from the Taliban stronghold?

D: Britain and the US performed admirably in the task to defend freedom and democracy for the free world. It's just that Arab nations are still in fear of bombs from the US and may retaliate without warning somewhere in the world, possibly still on US soil. Meanwhile, the Afghan people need adequate leadership from within their own ranks, and are still in danger of starving over the winter. They need both food and help in setting up a makeshift government, one without the Taliban leaders. The Taliban still considers itself in charge and many from the ranks will be signing up to posts within the new government unless they are eradicated, screened out for having had a Taliban role sometime or other. Their ideology is the same rhetoric we've heard before- that of hatred of the West, of Christians, of Jews, and a radical approach to that problem, that of annihilation of all others not like them.

M: Whew, Diana, that is scary, and a frightful similar to the Nazi camp from years ago. We can't let them gain power again can we?

D: No, not without drastic consequences. So whilst the nations, the United Nations plan for a future for Afghanistan, it would be wise to consider even outsiders as leaders for a time, until the people can begin to heal from the terror their own Taliban regime reigned upon them for so many years.

M: It does take years to heal from fear and pain in some instances, politically, socially, personally.

D: Indeed it does take time, and the people are so fearful now of doing anything. Afraid that the next government will be worse. I wish to say that there is nothing to fear now to them.

Except Osama Bin Laden and his cohorts. They are still finding ways to do terror and will if given the opportunity.

M: Di, if you don't mind my asking, have they left the country or where is Osama Bin Laden? That we'd all like to know.

D: He is in hiding in the caves still. He wishes to escape to perhaps one of the lesser Arab nations, and arrangements are in the works for this.

M: Do you know which one?

D: I can't really say or know, there are many who will give safe harbor. I wish not to say more about his whereabouts. He will be caught in time.

M: I want to say thank God for having saved the lives of our (US) aid workers, Dayna and Heather.

I received in prayer more than a month ago that they would be saved miraculously!

D: Indeed it was a miracle -their rescue. But you see they walk with God, and all who do will be saved in this life and in the next life as well. And so it is for all who walk with Him. We are rejoicing even here in Heaven for them.

M: Is that all for today Di?

D: I am concluding shortly. The world still needs prayer now, and for a time to come. Things are not as easy as they seem, now that the Taliban government has fallen. It will still take a miracle to deal with terrorists elsewhere in the Arab world and to change the way some of the extremists think, to bring about lasting hope for peace in the world now. Moderate Arab nations can do much now to refuse safe harbor to terrorists and to set the new role for Arab/Muslim nations to to do good, love others and not resort to crimes of bloodshed over religious differences.

I am asking all to come to prayer at this time of Thanksgiving in the United States and remember your friends and enemies alike. Give thanks too for your great abundance and do not forget those less fortunate than you. I am your consolation in a troubled time, Diana, Princes of Love.

Diana's Thanksgiving Message November 22, 2001

M: Diana, I heard you today. Did you want to say anything on Thanksgiving?

D: My pleasure always to use your voice, your willingness to bring forth my message.

It is just to say thank you to everyone for all the love they have shown in the past few months; and to say that more love, prayer and perseverance will be needed in the months ahead, both for the Afghan people and the world at large. The situation is far from over, and even when the evil doer is caught, the drama in the Middle East is not over. Dodi wishes to say that his people are frightened of the U.S. coming in and just bombing any Arab nation for whatever reason.

M: I'm sorry to hear this. I know just what he means. They are talking of taking on Iraq next.

D: Yes, and it may well lead to WWWIII if they don't slow down on the race to conquer the world.

M: History is a sad reminder, but the Crusades were a miserable failure to rid the world of Islamic militants a thousand years ago.

D: Well spoken, for this was my next thought. You see, you can't win people over to democracy by dropping bombs on them. This is not freedom. It is tyranny in the extreme. People the world over know that freedom comes forth from the people, as it says in the constitution of the United States and other constitutions of free nations. Nowhere does it say that freedom comes forth from dropping bombs and killing others who don't think like you do.

M: Thank you, Diana, for your words of compassion and kindness towards those who are in need of mercy at the moment. Perhaps those Arab nations will come to democracy at the hands of mad tyrants then?

D: Not at all, really. They will need assistance in dissembling the regimes of some of the Islamic militant nations, such as Iraq. To go in and bomb makes no sense when diplomacy — forceful diplomatic relations will do just as well. The people of Iraq are tired of the regime and will welcome aid and diplomacy. Give this a try before we have an all-out world war. The results could be miraculous and just what is needed in this tight dilemma we all face. At some point we have to sit down together and realize we are One World! Even those of us who are now at peace and at rest in heaven. You see that in heaven we are busy sending messages of light to the mass consciousness, to assist all on the path to heaven on Earth. Either of two things will come of this: we will co-create a heaven or co-create a hell. Can this choice amongst brothers everywhere be hard to choose for?

Who chooses hell but those bent on it? And why not choose for peaceful negotiation and helpful news to the lesser Arab nations instead of more bombs?

M: Diana, you are a brilliant Ambassador of peace for our planet. You've got my vote, and I agree.

When can we start? And, what can we do to get our government to agree to peaceful civilized negotiation?

D: You, my dear, are doing your part by listening and printing the words on your web site and in your new book. As to the world leaders, we are working round the clock to influence their thoughts, their aspirations to come to peace in alternative ways than war. With this thought I close for now. I send my light to you and all in powerful positions, as a brilliant ray of light for the human race now working, "behind the scenes" for the world. I am Diana, Ambassador of Light and Love for humanity, and I send my love onward to you!

M: Thank you, Diana.

"All You Need is Love" December 2, 2001

D: I wish to now resume my commentary on the political scene worldwide.

M: Yes, please go on, Diana.

D: It is with regret that we learned of the bombings in Jerusalem. Dodi is so sorry to hear of this, as it was hoped that our warnings not to attack Israel would be heeded.

He had said that more terror might bring down the leader of the PLO. That is what may happen now.

M: The worldwide situation is then worsening.

D: I am afraid so, for now. Though the situation appears to be worsening, I will still say that all are not to lose hope. That God and his angels and those in our dimension are watching over the world with love, and great sadness at this next tragedy.

M: I am wondering if all of this would have come about with Al Gore. Since he won the popular vote, and the vote was never allowed to be tallied, I wonder if his presidency would have been different.

D: You raise an interesting point, and your intuition may be correct, but for now that is only conjecture. I'm here to assist the human race move on from the standpoint of futile hatreds, war, killing and senseless acts of murder. Haven't we all had enough of this?

M: Diana, thank you, and well spoken. I certainly have. Is there anything else you wish to say at this juncture?

D: In the words of the Beatles, "All You Need is Love!"

M: Yes, so true. I'm saddened too at the loss of George Harrison.

D: Yes, he is in spirit now, that I confirmed earlier in the week. I wish to say that we've met and he's making his adjustment to spirit quite well now!

M: He was a spiritual type of guy, he knew a lot about this sort of thing. He can't be having that hard a time now that he is there. Is he with John Lennon as well?

D: They will meet again at an appointed time. George too influenced the magnetic grid surrounding earth, with his music. And he introduced a generation to Eastern religious tradition. He helped to shape an entire generation, and he will be remembered always for his contribution.

I wish to close with the thought that all we need is love. If we could all love enough for one moment, we would abolish war and killing from the planet. If we could all love enough we could eliminate so much unnecessary suffering. So, for those of you who are trying to live in love, I commend your efforts, know that love is never in vain. I ask all listening to my messages to love one another, and to continue in your efforts which are commendable. All my love at this time of sorrow,

Diana,
Princess of Love.

A Request for a Peace Accord December 9, 2001

M: Diana, what is it that you want or need? I am here to hear you.

D: Thank you my darling. I wish to continue on with some of the themes from yesterday.

D: You are loved by the many who are fortunate to know you.

M: Thanks Diana, for sending me Tasha, this child of light and love.

D: And I can attest that she is just that.

M: Diana, is there anything you wish to say at this time?

D: You are becoming an instrument of peace in this world on my behalf. I wish to say I am pleased that you are being accepted on the internet and in the new church group which is meeting. In time you will be overwhelmed with visitors and requests. At which time you will have to prioritize your time by selecting just those causes and people who are vibrating on your high level. And to eliminate those who are not in accordance with your evolving truth in spirit.

M: What a lovely compliment. I only hope to live up to it.

D: You will my Darling!

M: Diana, what do you make of the evolving situation in Afghanistan?

D: I am quite pleased really with things there, except for the continued bombing, which has to stop, because really now the manhunt for the terrorists is the crucial action.

M: Di, I know how you feel about the bombing, and all the useless suffering. Not to contradict you but I thought that they were bombing the caves near Tora Bora in hopes of finding Osama Bin Laden and the network of terrorists.

D: That is the agenda, and indeed they will succeed.

M: So then why are you against the bombing?

D: Purely from a humanitarian point of view my dear. I'm not at all opposed to the Allied Nations at this time. Many in Afghanistan are celebrating the victory of the Northern Alliance and the new found freedom. It is my ardent hope that the Allies don't go into Iraq or any other middle eastern nation to continue bombing. We are already in another crisis in Palestine/ Israel.

M: Diana, Dodi's words came back to haunt me about this. He said in an earlier channeling "Palestine, be warned, further terror will hurt your cause for a homeland, and take down your leader." Those were his words, certainly not mine.

D: Yes, they certainly were, and you did an excellent job trying to get the word out. It is unfortunate that more world leaders were not aware of the web site at the time of the message, which was however delivered on time. The situation in Palestine/Israel is really quite serious. While numerous talks are going on and ample time was given for Mr. Arafat to round up the terrorists, he really can't control all terror factions there now. I can attest to his interest in peace there and in his continued effort to create a homeland for his people. I wish to remind world leaders that Palestine has suffered much oppression, and that Israel really holds the upper hand politically, and therefore, so much damage in the press to Mr. Arafat has been done. It's not all his fault and he is doing all he can to arrest those terrorists who perpetrate these crimes against Israel. He deserves to be heard and so do the Palestinian people, who are suffering so greatly there. He only wishes to create the long promised homeland, and to stop the violence. He really is a good man, and should not be held in such contempt in the press for the actions of Hamas and Jihad. They are all throughout the region there and will be for some time. The nations must act now to create peace and a homeland for Palestine before this next crisis erupts into a major war in the region.

I am asking the Allied nations to come together at a peace accord, and try to assist Mr. Arafat and the Israelis to come to terms with one another without further bloodshed. In the name of your God, and in the interest of your children, and your children's children, this peace accord must succeed!

M: Beautifully spoken, may there be a peace accord and soon.

D: I wish to close by saying again that religion and holy wars must come to an end on this planet. **That religion is for the edification of the spirit and not for self-righteous**

service to the cause of holy war or any other violence. That religion and violence don't belong together, for they are not the will of God. I ask all good people everywhere to pray for peace in that region, and continue in their good efforts to comfort those afflicted by war and poverty. I commend your efforts everywhere and know that each little effort has a ripple effect, so that one by one, ripple by ripple we can effect change for good- for each heart and each mind- and thus transform the world.

All My love, Diana

Diana's Christmas Message December 16, 2001

M: Diana, I am here for you today. Is there anything on your mind at the moment?

D: I thought you'd never answer. But, gratefully you always do. I wish to continue in the same vein as last week's message, to stress continually that the nations of the world must renounce all violence. And to commend the speech and actions taken by Mr. Arafat at this time. He certainly did a lot to arrest the terrorists right amongst his own Palestinian people by arresting so many of Hamas and Jihad. This is highly commendable and will be seen in the eyes of many the seriousness of his plea for peace and for a homeland for Palestine.

M: I was pleased to see action taken against those two extremist organizations, and to see his continued efforts for peace. It strikes me more as a struggle for him than an effort, and in this I feel sorry for his people and him.

D: This is so true, they have been left without a home for so many years. It is up to the authorities now in Israel to recognize a Palestinian state. Without it I am afraid that there will be more of the same terror so prevalent throughout the Middle East!

M: Obviously, that will occur. When people are deprived they resort to crimes of terror out of sheer desperation. But each time, the terror tends to produce more terror instead of the desired political result.

D: Well spoken, my dearest. I think for now, I wish to say that all that Mr. Arafat has done is indeed highly commendable, and in time it may earn him his reputation back. Israel must stop the attacks on the Palestinian settlements. It is reeking havoc there.

M: And in the eyes of the Muslim world I am sure it must cause smoldering anger.

D: Indeed it has!

M: Di, I am wondering, is there any further threat of terror from the El Queda network? They were saying that they wanted to strike again to finish the month of Ramadan.

D: I am sorry to report that although the authorities feel there is no threat, there still is a very real one.

M: Can you be specific at all?

D: I am afraid I can't say for sure what if anything they wish to do. There are still many plots, and although one was thwarted, others are in the works. This time, they wish to strike with weapons of mass destruction. And they have some of them, only in small amounts. Lest you should worry I wish to say that what they have is significant, but their methods are inadequate.

M: So we should continue in vigilance while not worry too much?

D: That is correct and your authorities know where to look and to whom, lest they should desire to strike. I commend all the US intelligence authorities for being on to them, for they know.

M: Is that all for today, Diana?

D: Not quite really. I wish to move on to the light of the Christ this season of Christmas. That all of you have a divine spark within, that you are to nurture this spark, until the whole world is filled with light, the light of Christmas. That there really was a star that shone in the night sky so long ago, and all of us were there, visiting with Mary and the holy Child. That it was a true and real occurrence and it is yet another symbol from the Father, that we are all that light.[4] If we will but look within for our guidance, we shall not err. My light and blessings on all of you this Christmas, love Diana

---

[4]Eide, Rita, *Celestial Voice of Diana*: Her Spiritual Guidance to Finding Love. In this channeled account, Diana says that she was the mother of the Virgin Mary in another incarnation. We may then assume that she traveled to Bethlehem to visit Mary and Jesus, the holy child. In light of that, I find her words here fascinating, while I understand that some will find past lives difficult to accept.

3. Diana at Christmas, watercolor, Marcia McMahon ©2001.

Diana is in her red gown for a Christmas celebration in Norway. It was at this time she learned she was pregnant for a second time, with Harry. To view this watercolor in color, go to: www.angelfire.com/mb2/diana_speaks/gallery_index.html/**diana_speaks/**

The Christ Within December 22, 2001

M: I'm here for you Diana.

D: Thank you my darling.

M: Is there anything on your mind for today?

D: Today I wish to address the continuing issues of the Middle East, specifically Palestine, and also the emerging government in Afghanistan. Mr. Arafat has done a commendable job in cleaning up the Hamas and Jihad organizations in Israel. When is Israel going to negotiate for peace there? After all, the people of Palestine have been waiting for forty years! We, Dodi and I, would like world leaders to acknowledge the presence of Mr. Arafat as official leader and the World Powers (Allied Nations and Arab Nations) to then put pressure on Israel to get the peace process or cease-fire negations moving along. This is crucial for peace in the region, and in the eyes of the Arab world. They need to see progress and this indeed will deter terror in the region.

M: Brilliant as always, Diana!

D: Thank you. I am honored to do this work and in a short time you'll have just those readers who need to see these messages on the web site reading this!

M: That's good. I've felt discouraged all day about the low visitation.

D: It's Christmas and so many are so busy bustling around looking for things! If only they would instead look within, to their source, the Christ within. So much last minute shopping is such a waste of time. I say this because I in fact wasted so much time doing just the same thing; shopping! I lived for it at one time in my life! Now, neither clothes nor appearance matter in the least. But all is as it should be and I was to reach millions through my image as a feminine mystique. And I enjoyed the role I played in fashion as well as in my later charitable work. It really laid the groundwork for my work in the afterlife now, as Ambassador for Peace. So many worldwide trust my good name. And I am so honored this is as it should be.

M: Wow, Diana, you again have said a wondrous amount of wisdom!

D: Now I wish to return to world affairs. It seems that things are winding down for Afghanistan, and that the new government will soon emerge. While it is excellent that the Taliban regime is toppled, be aware that the Al Queda network is still operative under cover in other Arab nations. That they are still plotting.

M: What kind of plots? And what should our intelligence be looking for?

D: The weapons of mass destruction! They hope to use them soon on U.S. cities! Bombs filled with chemicals, dumped out on cites, as well as nuclear warheads. They want annihilation of the West, particularly due to the success in weeding out the Taliban.

M: Is this Iraq? Or is this another part of the Al Qaeda network?

D: They are all in it together, different factions wanting different things. **I urge the authorities of the United States to take cover and appropriate action ahead of time. This is why your President needs the new program of warheads. To fend off bombs! It is imperative that all intelligence sources be brought together to turn the tide of terror. It can be done if enough warning is allowed, as well as shutting down Al Qaeda and the storehouse of weapons in Iraq.**

M: Di, I thought you opposed our going in there to Iraq?

D: I did, but under the circumstances, I am now reversing my opinion. They have the warheads and they must be dealt with! **It is imperative to get intelligence operational in Iraq!**

M: Di, what do you want me to do with this information? It seems so "hot." How can I, a common U.S. citizen, deal with this and get it to the right people? I feel this is a little crazy. Giving me this information and then asking me to deliver the letter. Where? To whom?

D: You will soon see. Trust the Holy Spirit, who watches over us all!

M: Is that all for today Di?

D: I am afraid so. I see you are growing weary so I'll stop for a time. I want you to rest. And rest in the arms of love, for all of you who read this, Your Creator God watches over all of you at this crucial time, and will not allow this to happen to your world. May peace be our only objective, our only thought, our only hope at this time,

All my love, Diana.

Princess Diana's Message December 29, 2001

M: Diana, I am here to be your voice today.

D: My great pleasure always, to speak through you.

M: Di, is there any issue which you wish to address today?

D: There is, of course, an agenda as always!

M: Oh, good, I look forward to your discourse!

D: Today, I would like to address the increasing tensions in the Pakistani and Indian areas.

M: Yes, Di, I have been worried that all-out war might break out there at any time.

D: As you might have suspected the Al Qaeda network has been behind much of the confusion there, and instigated the violence at the Parliament in India. I must make clear that the Pakistani government had nothing to do with that. In fact Osama Bin Laden has cleverly devised a diversion plan so that while he is in hiding there (Pakistan), the attention will be diverted to the other border, releasing millions of troops from the North now to the South in Pakistan.

M: Wow! You said a mouthful! Now, Diana, I had trouble getting the last word out on your behalf, and now you give me the approximate whereabouts of Bin Laden and that he orchestrated this tension between the two countries! It gets even more difficult being your channel.

D: Don't lose heart, my dear Darling one! I love your work and all that you are doing on behalf of peace for the world. Dodi and I are most grateful. We do want more people to see the message.

Dodi says he feels it's crucial to get the word to the Muslim world, where they will see the prophetic nature of his words about Israel as well as his advice for them (Muslims), so that there will be no more terror or violence in the name of the blessed Allah.

M: Again Diana, I am honored to be of use to you. But I must confess the difficult nature of this as it borders on intelligence and I can't handle that red hot stuff!

D: You won't need to I'll be showing you how to get it out anonymously on certain web sites.

M: Now that we know the truth wouldn't it be interesting to present this tidbit of information to Pakistan or India, for them to realize that they were duped into these near war positions by the enemy!

D: That is indeed what happened! We want the world to know that it was the work of the mastermind, Bin Laden. And not the doing of Pakistan. Mr. Musharraf has been doing a commendable job of ridding his country of terrorists, but he can't do it all at one time. At the same time, there are those within his country who are now harboring the terrorists and doing so quite willingly. The government should be on to them by now, but they're slow to realize just what a platform bin Laden really had in Pakistan.

M: Di, it would be a shame to have all-out war when the reason is so blatantly wrong in the first place.

D: Correct, the world doesn't need more war right now. Afghanistan is just getting reorganized.

The West, particularly Britain and the US must continue a policy of capturing Bin Laden for he is indeed the mastermind behind so many of these apparent plots!

M: My conscience always seems to say, get these words out, yet I can't bring myself to send them to the government. I just can't be involved with them, besides they don't accept psychic messages.

D: All the easier to send it on, because they don't have to believe it, just get the words, the message. Even if it is regarded as nothing more than a tip or a delusional thing, which of course , it most certainly is not!

M: I am most honored to do this work, although it does present problems. Is that all for today, Diana?

D: I'm not closing just yet. I wish to say that although it seems that the war in Afghanistan is over, and we are relived, your President is right when he calls for justice for Bin Laden. The terrorists will be brought to justice! God will not let their agenda prevail! I want to wish everyone peace in the New Year, and with the concerted help of many who work for peace, you included, we want to continue to hold the precious jewel the Earth in the God Light, and hope for peace in this New Year.

Your continued prayers for peace are requested by the many on this side, and they are felt in the magnetic grid surrounding your Earth. Therefore do not loose heart, you who work for peace!

For we are doing all we can in spirit, to bring just that one desire of mens' hearts everywhere to peace!

Let peace reign, my love, Diana

Diana, Eternal Voice of Love January 5, 2002

M: I'm here for you, so speak through me if you

D: My great pleasure always.

M: Any topic or agenda for today?

D: First, don't feel discouraged about the book study, *The Celestial Voice of Diana: Her Guidance to Finding Love,* by Rita Eide. You've sent word out to the papers, and at church, and even though the minister is not understanding your work, or clearly it's validity, she will in time.

M: You mean, when I am published or sooner than that?

D: I'll see to it through the many who will be telling her about your course, and this is what you are to concentrate on, even though you have so many pressures with school right now. School isn't as important as peacemaking. And that's what we're here to do. So without further adieu, we'll begin.

Today I wish to address the increasing pressures around the world that things need to be brought to peace with regards Palestine! If only your leaders will focus on just that one issue so much suffering can be averted through diplomacy alone!

M: I saw where the US sent an ambassador to begin negotiations with Palestine and Israel. I think we're all a little tired of all the violence there. I just wonder, once they get the state of Palestine if they'll ever get along!

D: Indeed, it seems impossible, but it isn't. Justice begins in the heart chakra, and that is where both parties, Mr.

Arafat and Mr. Sharon need to feel compassion for one another's plight.

M: Indeed, instead of all that blame they are constantly finger pointing like children.

D: Exactly, and we as a world all need to grow up and learn to treat one another with respect and dignity instead of deception, violence and greed. Fairness is something that nations as well as persons need to practice, those virtues we all cherish and strive to make part of our daily vocabulary.

M: I certainly do. Fairness is hard in an unfair world, sometimes it seems as though I go out of my way to be fair and find myself unfairly treated in many situations still. Why is that Diana?

D: Fairness is in the heart chakra. One must feel fairness and the ability to understand the other. So few are in touch with their emotions of the heart. So it's hard for them to be fair. They are what you call "hard". Your heart tells you when you are doing something detrimental to another and those of us who follow our heart, have no trouble in life with how we treat others. But we can't ask those who aren't as evolved as we are to feel in their hearts what damage they are doing. If they felt it for even one moment, they wouldn't do it any longer.

The situations in the Middle East are just exaggerated children's games. They feel no mercy for those who lose their life in suicide bombings or for those who are invaded by Israeli tanks. This they get to view in full detail when they reach our side, and see the sickness and horror they inflict on innocent lives. This violence has to stop! The human race must now more than ever, reach forth a helping hand, and a heart of mercy for those of whatever "other" side there is. It is indeed the only way to peace. Open your heart chakra more and you will begin to notice the feelings of others toward you, and other miracles as well.

M: Diana those are wonderful words of wisdom and I feel that we all need to open our hearts when we get confused and defensive about how others treat us.

D: I do know how it feels to be under pressure to perform tasks and work with the public in a meaningful way. Sometimes just the slightest gesture of kindness, the word of mercy or a handshake can be so much to someone who is suffering.

M: Di, I've seen you in all the pictures comforting the dying, the lonely, the elderly, the afraid. You are an inspiration to me, and to many. You certainly had the art of comfort and upliftment. It's a little harder when dealing with those who are being ugly for no apparent reason.

D: Oh, I've plenty of experience dealing with them too. It takes a self-determination and confidence that what you are all about is goodness, love, and light. Nothing can stop me now, just as they couldn't stop me when I was living. They think they shut me up, but now I've channels like you all over the world bringing forth a different aspect of myself in such a way as to more powerfully convey the very essence of me, which of course was love. I was the Princess of Love and still am, forever more.

I am Diana, eternal voice of love!

Have Faith in Miracles! January 12, 2002

M: Diana, I'm here to be your voice today. Is there anything on your mind?

D: It will become increasingly important that you accept with faith your work. You need to overcome doubt with faith. Too much doubt can stall your efforts to get my words out on the web.

M: I know, there is so much ignorance of this sort of thing, and yet, when people read the words, see your picture, it works like magic, for them to see this magnificence coming from as it were, Diana, the Princess.

D: You must have faith in miracles and in this miracle even as we speak.

M: I do, it just wavers a bit, from time to time. And I have to be your spokesperson, and you were loved but also a controversial figure. It's not the easiest thing representing you publicly, you know.

D: I only know too well, my darling friend, of your difficulties of late with the minister and the church, as well as in your own family. I have been through that with families!

M: Don't we know it! But, is there something that you wish to address today?

D: I so wish to commend Mr. Musharraf for his excellent speech on the insidious effects of terrorist propaganda being spread by Muslim fundamentalists in his own country. He is extremely brave to come out against them, as they are always plotting something insidious and devious against him!

M: Isn't it time we as a human race woke up to the possibilities of religious tolerance and correct interpretation of the scriptures, including the Quran? After all, he said the Jihad was against ignorance and fear, and he is so right.

D: Well spoken, my dearest. You're getting to sound like me in this more and more. Your use of words and diplomacy are evidencing themselves!

M: Well, I'm very complimented. After all, I do take a certain amount of criticism with this job, you know?

D: I know and I'm afraid I can't promise you an easy ride through this troubled time that the world is going through. Without your voice, it would be much more grim.

M: I have some questions for you. How do you suppose I ought to get the words out anonymously to those in positions of power, say heads of state or diplomats?

D: You've been doing a commendable job of sending this message to web sites that are open to channeling. **As to the diplomatic side of this message, this is where Dodi and I feel that you must seek out those people through their web sites and send anonymous emails so as to convey our**

messages while keeping your own privacy. In this way, they will see the words and not have to worry about how they appeared before them on the page. Did I say to have faith in miracles?

Then this will be seen by just those few individuals who I point out to you. You may find the web sites and then send the messages, hopefully using another name as well.

This will not change the credibility of my message because it's my good name that precedes you.

M: Thank you, once again Diana for your perfect explanation. I'll do my best then to send these things on anonymously.

D: You are most welcome. We are well aware of your feelings of conscience regarding this important information and its contents do need to reach the very top people!

M: Is that all for today then Diana?

D: I am concluding shortly. I wish to personally thank you for your fearlessness in this critical time. And for trying so hard to get this message out! When the book is published much more awareness for it will be there. Many thousands will know of it, and your good work. Meanwhile, continue steadfast in your efforts. My love to you and all who do good works in this critical time of so much change. Have faith in miracles, for they will be sent to you, and to those who read these words. My loving presence with you all.

Diana,

Princess of Love!

A Formula for Peace January 19, 2001

M: I'm here for you, Diana. Is there anything you wish to speak on today?

D: Thank you, my darling. As always, there are things I wish to address. Must the continued hatreds and attacks continue in Israel/Palestine? So much violence and suffering there could be averted with proper placement of the State of Palestine. People have wandered there for more than forty years. Isn't it time to give them a homeland? After all, this is what so much of the bloodshed is all about!

M: Yes, I saw on the news about the bombing of the radio station. That Israel came in, evacuated the building, and blew it right up. How can Israel just do that and still remain the good guy in the eyes of the United States?

D: It is a wonder, really. Isn't it time humanity stopped this childish violence and grew up in its ways of coping with differences! This has been my message for months now on the web site and the new book emerging. That mankind, must, if it is to continue, learn ways other than violence to solve political and geographical problems. So much unnecessary suffering could have been adverted if our messages of light were heeded. So few are getting these messages, and at the same time, they will be seen by just those individuals who need them.

M: As you can see, I am doing my best but it is no easy dilemma getting this word out.

D: Your efforts, however small, are greatly appreciated by those of us in the light of God.

M: I will try harder to reach the top people, as you had suggested. But of course, the terrorist groups will do what they want and aren't reading these messages or any messages of light.

D: No, but top diplomats need to see my words, and feel the truth conveyed in them.

M: I will do my best.

D: And you always do! Now, I wish to say to those who are working on matters of peacemaking in the Middle East and Afghanistan, that your job isn't easy. That there are many political factions that want things to stay status quo. But that should not deter your steadfast efforts at peacemaking. This is indeed one of the only things that has to be done in order to save the world from itself, possible nuclear annihilation. Peacemaking in this region will ensure a safer world, while allowing the violence to continue will worsen the world wide tensions! So many of the Arab nations are feeling threatened with possible bombs. And this is not the way to peace. Diplomatic efforts need to be tried first before resorting to bombs!

M: Obviously, Di, this seems the way to do this. But the people have gone mad. They aren't able to respond with reason, they seem hell bent on bombs and killing over there.

D: It's sad really. My heart goes out to the innocent whose lives are lost or forever maimed by these senseless acts.

M: Is there anything else for today?

D: I'm concluding shortly. **We and Dodi wish to see a cease-fire in Israel and negotiations resume quickly. That all need to work together for peace for the sake of our children, and our children's children! The State of Palestine needs to co-exist alongside Israel, and a map needs to be drawn up, and adhered to. The people of Palestine deserve this, and need to feel acknowledged in their right for a Homeland. Without this, I am afraid that the conditions under which everyone is living will continue in the terror hold. We ask that Mr. Sharon and Mr. Arafat come together with the aid of the diplomacy of the United States to found the state of Palestine, and stop holding off on it!**

We in spirit realm take no sides in the dispute but merely offer our concerted help to those still in manifestation. So that a world will behold a rose of Sharon, where once bloodshed was!

In closing then, I wish to say that this transmission of light is from the light worker, Diana, Princess of Love, who asks that you live in love and peace.

2. **Diana Among the Cosmos** © 2001,watercolor by Marcia McMahon.

This is one of my first interpretations of Diana. I used flowers from my fall garden and incorporated them around Diana.

Cosmos seemed particularly appropriate, since she is a cosmic being of light. To view this painting in color go to www.angelfire.com/mb2/diana_speaks/gallery_index.html/ and go to Diana Gallery I.

Diana's Message to Elton John January 26, 2002

M: Di, I'm here for you today. Is there anything you wish to speak about?

D: Well, of course there is an agenda. Today, I wish to address the increasing tensions in Israel Palestine, and to say again that this violence and hatred must stop! That humanity must live in mutual cooperation and trust. I am asking again that Mr. Arafat and Mr. Sharon, with the help of the United States and Britain, come together for peace talks and cease-fire.

M: Di, I saw what the Israelis did to Mr. Arafat. Their tanks surrounded around his house. That is outrageous that the International community is tolerating this latest personal attack on him!

D: We don't take sides in spirit. We merely advise what the desired outcome of this situation could be. Obviously, Mr. Arafat's human rights are being violated. And this level of aggression must stop!

On both sides, the mutual hatreds have to stop in order that order be restored. Israel isn't doing anyone any good by their overt aggressions, but neither are the many suicide bombings that persist in the region. Mr. Arafat has come out against this tide of terror in his own country. His own countrymen aren't listening. They are fed up and feel that terror is the only way. **There will indeed be many more plots of terror on the US soil if the state of Palestine isn't worked for and created. So much of this needless suffering could be averted if the authorities in the region come together**

for a cease-fire, for peace and for Palestine as a recognized state. I must stress that this is the solution to the crisis!

M: That is brilliant, Diana. And I agree, and only now have I come to see the actual need of the Palestinian state so clearly.

D: I am relieved that so much of the bombing and warfare is winding down in Afghanistan. We just don't want to see the next war right there in the Middle East.

On a more personal note, I wish to thank Elton John, my dear friend for all he's done in his music and song to support my causes and charities in the world. (The Diana, Princess of Wales Memorial Fund, and the AIDS fund) Even since my passing, he has been active, and to let him know that all is forgiven here on this side. He's a brilliant artist with a similar path to mine, and that is why we were close friends. That he too, is an overcomer and a master of great music!

M: Is that all for today, Diana?

D: You are to be commended for your courage this week in sending these messages of light on to the right sources and people. I wish this to continue until such time as it is no longer needed, and our world is transformed into a world of light! That this message of mine reach the very top people involved in this crisis, because they will recognize my voice and my message as genuine. That I am watching over all of you with care, and am a light worker here in spirit for the benefit of humanity at this time. My love to all who work for peace,

Diana

Diana and Dodi Call for a Peace Accord Feb 4, 2002

M: Di, I am here now, to be your voice.

D: Thank you Darling, I knew you wouldn't forget me.

M: Is there any topic you wish to cover today?

D: I wish you to not feel depressed about those who don't understand your important work. That this will soon change, and they will feel foolish for having been so harsh with you, for your work in listening to my voice, on behalf of peace, is divinely appointed and they can't stop you.

M: Thanks Di, I am easily comforted, it only takes one person sometimes to see the beauty, the worth, the value in someone or something.

D: That is so true. Now, I'd like to move to world affairs and have some things to say.

M: Ok, go on.

D: That I am still asking the top diplomats of the US to go into Israel and Palestine, and be fearless. Begin peace negotiations. An immediate cease-fire will need to happen first. Mr. Arafat is doing all he can to control his countrymen. That they are acting out violence in their own ways, without his permission. It might be wise or possible for the United Nations to step in and provide Peace Keeping troops in the entire region. And Mr. Sharon needs to assume some responsibly for stopping the tanks and assaults on the Palestinian settlements.

M: Those are all excellent ideas, Di. I really think that a peace keeping force there might help. But who would want to staff it? It seems anyone could be the target there. That is why I haven't ever considered sending even an email message like this, because it is so darned bloody and hateful.

D: Indeed it is! And the violence must come to an end. For the sake of your children, and your children's children. If there is to be an Earth as we know it, I plead with all those powerful nations, especially the US and Britain to pursue this path of peace before more violence erupts on US soil!

M: Is that what they're planning again?

D: Of course, as always! **They want weapons of mass destruction used as quickly as possible on US cities; and they have them!**

M: If, however, they suddenly found the US involved in peace negotiations, they might not do this right?

D: That is entirely correct, although some factions are more prone to violent thinking anyway.

I am closing shortly. I wish to say that both Dodi and I are asking the top diplomats to find a way to meet soon, over this very issue. It could very well turn the tide of terror that is still being planned for the US, and in this way solve many problems at one time. As you say in your world, everything is easier in hindsight. Well, we in spirit have both foresight and hindsight, and can see the possible results of doing nothing, and the possible result of world peace even in the Middle East if enough pressure is exerted on both Israel and Palestine and their respective leaders. There is still hope for the world as we speak, and we hope that this advice from spirit is acted upon in a practical way. We send on our love, light and blessings to the peace workers and light workers of the world.

Our love, Diana and Dodi

Princess Margaret is Welcome Home Feb 9, 2002

M: Diana, I'm here to be your voice. Forgive my lapse in faith in myself.

D: You are doing fine, all things considered. As I told you, your friend who is in spirit is in the resting place and wishes not to be disturbed for a time. At the same time, you have already noticed his thoughts within yours, so you know beyond a doubt that in time, you will hear from him. It is best with newly departed souls to let them rest in peace as it says on your stones. And you are doing as well as can be expected with such a loss.

M: I'm so sorry to hear of Princess Margaret, Di.

D: Yes, I confirm that she is now in spirit here amongst us all. She is welcome home!

M: Was there anything you wished to comment on today. I am trying to remain open to your words.

D: There is an aura of depression and loss around you, and it is best to wait until you are more emotionally clear to channel. We send you our healing light at this time. And we'll meet again tomorrow when you're feeling better.

M: Thanks, Di.

Note: Diana is always sensitive to my personal life. At this juncture I had learned of the death of an old boyfriend, and I was greatly saddened. I am so appreciative that Diana only uses me as a channel when I'm at my best. She in fact, insists that I be emotionally and mentally clear to channel.

Commence the Peace Accord! Feb 10, 2002

M: Di, I'm here for you today.

D: Thank you darling. There is much I wish to speak on.

M: Ok, go on.

D: The increasing tensions in the Middle East need everyone's attention. It is not enough that your president met with Aerial Sharon, and mentioned the horrible conditions of the Palestinians. He needs to come full out with Mr. Sharon and ask for the negotiations for the state of Palestine to begin. This is imperative for world order, stability in the region and the world. As I said before, the US must be seen as advocate to the lesser Arab nations, Palestine in particular, in order to win the war on terror. Terror falls away naturally when the needs of the oppressed are being addressed and met.

M: Your point is well taken Di. I agree with your opinion. And I know you can see more there in spirit than we can here.

D: I bow to all the royalty who are doing this important work. For you are the true royals! And I salute you in spirit. I ask that all those diplomats and other peace workers put pressure on the President of the United States, and on Mr. Blair, to commence this Peace Accord. It will succeed where others failed, if only to acknowledge Mr. Arafat at a time when his popularity is waning.

M: I remember Dodi's words of warning about further terror on Israel.

D: Yes, it is so true. Dodi's words were there for all who would listen, and we wish to see more Muslims on your web site. To understand that we represent them, and the Allied forces in this situation and we take no sides. We want to achieve our goal of peace for the world, so that all may live in harmony and peace. And this is the will of most people everywhere!

M: So, again, it's the leaders who wage war, not so much the people.

D: This is not entirely so, as you see from the many terrorist attempts upon the US both within its borders and elsewhere. They feel there is a unity of Islam over them, but it is pure rhetoric in the extreme. There is no holy war, and Allah does not condone such action.

M: Di, is there any other agenda for today?

D: I am closing shortly. I want you to know that your friend is being looked after in the spirit realm. He has his guides to help him.

M: I've been praying for his soul, that he make the adjustment to afterlife.

D: That is excellent since all souls need help in this way, at the point of death. We are here to assist in that work. And we have assigned him guides, some whom he has known before, and some whom he has not met. He will be well in time. We ask you not to grieve so much for him, since you had released him many years ago. We wish you not to be in depression due to this, so that your important work will go on.

M: Thank you Diana, I'm so comforted to know his guides are there and others you sent. I'll do my best to release this person.

D: Now then, I want you to send this out to more diplomats than the one who is receiving my words at this time. They are reaching him, and influencing his great work. He is balanced enough to recognize my words are genuine, and can accept the help that is being offered. Now, find the others who knew me, and reach them with this one message, and know that your work as my channel for peace for the world is not in vain. I bow to you now, in spirit, as I salute all who work for peace, whether in my name, Diana of Wales, or in another's name. **We love you, we bless you, we beseech you, create a Palestinian State, and let grievances go, for the sake of your children, and your children's' children, so that we all may know the joy of human company! My love endures always,**

Diana,

Princess of Love

A Call to a Peace Accord Feb 17, 2002

M: Di, I'm here for you.

D: Yes, and now your vibration is much better, so then, we'll begin!

M: Yes and thank you for your remarks yesterday.

D: Sure, my darling friend!

M: Is there anything on your agenda today?

D: As always, I have one, and we best get moving on it. It had always been my pleasure when on Earth to assist people in crisis, and to lend a helping hand. It is in this same vein now that I am continuing my work on behalf of the many who will soon hear of your book and of your important peace work with me. That this is indeed true, that when we move on into the greater realms of light, we continue as we were, at the point where we had evolved to. So it should not be a surprise to learn that this is Diana, Princess of Wales, doing this good work for the sake of your Earth at this crucial time. There is much to be done, to create a better world.

M: Diana, are you still going to world affairs?

D: I'll be commenting on that shortly. I wish to say that unless the world powers all sit down at negotiations, the tensions in Israel and Palestine will worsen. We have seen another bloody weekend, with more suicide bombings, and now tanks and earth movers encamped all around the Palestinian people. It is a crisis over there and your US leaders and leaders from Britain must now commence the cease-fire and peace accord. All will agree, due to the strife and tension there. It is so important to at least invite the leaders, Arafat and Sharon or their representatives, to come to table and at least begin. I'm asking the heads of state not to ignore this situation and not to blame Mr. Arafat for further terror. He has asked and asked his people, they just feel desperate to control their lives. Mr. Sharon for his part needs to exercise restraint and stop the tanks now!

M: Diana, I do see what you're getting at. It could be all-out war soon, which could lead to world war if something isn't done to stop the carnage and the retaliation. All of your ideas have been sent on to the diplomats you suggested, and they do seem to have a different take on the situation, say other than the President. But, they can't wave a magic wand.

D: I am well aware of the difficulty your leaders have in this delicate matter, and that their opinions may differ as to the how to get the job done. I am asking again that the heads of State of the Allied powers call upon Mr. Arafat and Mr. Sharon, to set up a peace accord in another area, perhaps besides the US or Palestine, a neutral zone for a time.

M: I'll certainly send on messages, that is all I can do, Di.

D: Yes, and even seeing **my words will be of further help to turn the tide of terror that is now being planned for the United States, who is being seen as an ally to Israel in**

the process. If this perception persists it will, and has in the past, been the source of terror upon US soil. There is a unity amongst them they believe is Islam, but it is pure rhetoric in the extreme, as I have repeatedly said.

Nonetheless, if the US is serious about ending further terror, the way is being shown you here and now, which is decidedly different than all had thought. We in spirit see terrible agendas of the terrorists which can happen at any minute to the US.

M: Di, can you give me any idea what their line of attack might be at this point?

D: The annihilation of major US cities with weapons of mass destruction! That is why the peace accord on behalf of the state of Palestine is crucial to stop the terror now. Without some gesture of peace, I am afraid that so much more damage will be inflicted on innocent lives in the US.

I further wish to thank all the diplomats open to my words — for they are receptive. They are the true royalty at this time, and I bow to all peace workers!

I am Diana, a royal peace worker for the cause of Earth and its people.

Peace Proposal for the Mid-East Feb 23, 2002

M: Diana, I am here for you finally.

D: Yes, thank you. There is an agenda, a rather pressing one at that. I'm delighted to be in spirit with you now.

M: My honor, Diana, as always. Do go on.

D: I wish to further address, in as many ways possible, the continuing hatreds in the region of Israel/Palestine, to ask that the United Nations act now to save a future for both those countries. It would be best to have the full support of the United States and Britain, but as it stands the demands of Israel can't be the only demands being heard. The demands of the Palestinians must be heard as well. To put a demand that the terrorists, suicide bombers, stop their behavior is not possible. Mr. Arafat has no real control over the terrorists there. To assume he does is to misplace responsibility. He does not sanction terror, and does not stand for it. It is the responsibility of the terrorists themselves, not him.

M: You're right Diana. What I did not know is that Mr. Kofi Annan is seeing the worsening crisis there and is working on a plan. What is amazing to me is that just last week you mentioned a UN Peacekeeping force there, and that is precisely what may come out of this. I am going to try and find someone there I can send this message on to.

D: Brilliant! They know the plight of the Palestinian people, and of course the people in Israel who also suffer greatly from this terror inflicted upon them so needlessly.

When the cause for terror is eliminated, (by creating a Palestinian state), then there is no further reason to fear. There will be so much rejoicing when this happens.

M: Do you see the state of Palestine, or just a lessening of the terrorist bombings and tanks?

D: Well, since you asked, we in spirit can view possibilities. With a Palestinian state, we see a very bright future for the world. Without one, we may not see a world; or a world shattered by bombs, nuclear as well as biological terror.

M: There is so much at stake here, really.

D: So much and so much unnecessary suffering and hopelessness.

M: Di, is there anything else you wish to add to today's message?

D: I am closing shortly. I wish to say that if the United Nations will gather representatives from both Palestine and Israel together and also send in the Peacekeepers, that much more terror will be averted. Secondly, that the United States send Mr. Colin Powell or the President himself go to the peace accords, so that they may begin. There is so much good that can come from this and a possible stop to all the hatreds and bloodsheds which are happening now.

M: Can we ever reeducate ourselves as a world, so that people will know not to hate based on religion, based on fear?

D: The religious leaders would benefit to follow their own religious teacher instead of swaying people with rhetoric. So many of the religions of the world are so intent on their own doctrine. Saying they have the only truth. What if they knew that Dodi is with me in heaven? What if they knew that Muslims, Jews and Catholics are now with me in spirit, and that the religion they practiced on Earth didn't qualify them for heaven as much as their own integrity in their respective lifetimes. In the words of the great lyric poet John Lennon, "The world shall live as One," is the message here. Any religion which does not teach the oneness of all brothers isn't a religion of truth. We are all here in heaven! And we wish to remind our readers of this happy fact!

M: Is there anything else for today, Di?

D: I am closing shortly. I so wish to thank all the diplomats for being open to my words. I am influencing their thoughts as I do come through yours. Please give them my compliments, especially Mr. Powell! In time, many thousands more will know of my work in the afterlife, as Diana, Peace Worker for the world. I send you all my blessings of peace at this time, as we hold out hope for peace in the Middle East. I salute and bow to all the royalty who are doing the peace work for now.

My love, Diana

Diana Calls Upon the Great Leaders of Our Time Feb 25, 2002

M: Diana, I'm here for you now, today.

D: Thank you my darling. Did you enjoy our visit the other night?

M: I was thrilled. It seems you were in my dreams as well.

D: Now then I wish to move on.

M: OK, Di, do go on.

D: The situation in the Middle East still needs our attentions. That the leaders there and our Allied forces here need to take up the cause for peace, as His Royal Highness Prince Abdullah from Saudi Arabia has offered. **He has gotten wind of our ideas, as I said we send our thoughts to try to influence those diplomats that are open to peace.** I want all listening to my messages to take up his offer, while there is still time! He has suggested a brilliant plan, one which can be made to work. Why let one more innocent life be taken? Step forth now to show your leadership!

M: Didn't he say to create the State of Palestine, using the old 1967 boarders, and to draw it up, and to bring in the UN peacekeeping forces? I think that is brilliant, and very much the same request we've heard from you.

D: Yes, my request remains the same, no matter the situation. Until peace is found you'll hear my voice for a Peace Accord Now!

M: It's been the same for about six weeks now, and I'm praying the world leaders will act on this now.

D: It's our ardent prayer from here, spirit side, that this Peace Accord go forth with the help of the UN, the Saudi Prince Abdullah and with Mr. Sharon and Mr. Arafat, or their representatives. We wish to say that if this is done now, and a cease-fire put into place, that this time it would not be wise of Mr. Arafat to walk away from the boarders being drawn, and that he would have nothing to fear. That he will get a better deal this time, due to the immense pressure the international community would have on this to go forth. The world's future is at stake, as is the security and wellbeing of the entire United States, whose lives will be threatened without this Accord.

M: I've heard that before, are you still in reference to the bioterror or chemical weapons?

D: That and more, possibly nuclear weapons as well. When the reasons for terror are eliminated, there is nothing to fear.

M: Thank you Diana. Is there anything else for today?

D: I know how redundant I must sound to you and all who receive these messages! It's so important right now, and I wish there were a better way to communicate these messages, but acting as my channel, you're doing a wonderful job getting these messages out. And that is the **best that you can do.** Now I am calling on the International Community, Mr. Annan, Mr. Powell, Mr. Blair, Mr. Bush and all who care to make this world a better place to go to table, make arrangements and don't let this important opportunity for the world's children, and their children, pass you by.

My love and prayers for peace, Diana, the royal peace worker.

Create Palestine! March 2, 2002

M: Di, I 'm here to be your voice.

D: Thank you my darling.

M: I was very discouraged to see that the peace messages you gave mid-week, with the Saudi Prince as the focus, didn't go anywhere yet.

D: I'm extremely saddened at this point. It's so important that this peace accord come together. It's very difficult for all sides, I realize, but we were counting on the other diplomats to realize the importance of an Accord, and to get the peace process started again.

M: I'm so sorry more people didn't get the messages, or if they did, they didn't act on them.

D: Dearest don't be sorry. Obviously there are going to be roadblocks to success in any venture. This you know from your own experience. **What I wish to say now is that those same diplomats need to come together and have the peace Accord. Create the state of Palestine, before more terror breaks out on US soil!** It's imperative to have this in place, and to get going on it. For the terrorists will strike again without any action, I'm afraid to say.

M: Di, it's depressing. The Saudi Prince came forth and made some people think, even offered, and no one took his bid. Then we hear of alternate governments in place in case they nuke Washington, D.C.

D: I am so saddened at this juncture, that the leaders can't agree to an Accord. Some feel that it's the fault of Mr.Arafat, but really he can't control his countrymen. That this needn't be. All of this senseless violence, we see them coming over in spirit every day. Young and innocent people of all faiths, their lives are senselessly taken from them.

M: Diana, I believe your messages and want you to continue in your efforts, even if you feel that we've had a setback in policy. You can't just quit speaking simply because they haven't followed your advice. They have agendas, things that are hampering them.

D: Thank you, you are most kind to say those words right now. I wish to say that we had a wonderful opportunity for peacemaking for the state of Israel/Palestine, and to all diplomats getting these messages, that the world will fare much better if all will go to table and work toward this goal. No matter how long, no matter how difficult it seems. Do not let this opportunity go by. It may not come again. I hate to mention what I am seeing in spirit as a possibility for all Americans.

M: Diana, it would help us prepare if you can say. I sense your great sadness —Diana what is it, can you tell me?

D: I'm afraid that many thousands of lives will be given up to terror on the airplanes again, this time, in the form of the weapons of mass destruction!

That this need not be, if only our governments will come to the Peace Accord for Palestine!

M: Is there any particular country where we should look?

D: Their organization is worldwide terrorism, and to pin point a single nation might mean trouble to these countries. Your intelligence operations are well aware of this current threat and the country from which it stems. **If you are serious about preventing another terrorist attack, take a pro-active cause, and liberate Palestine!** It may reverse this terrible agenda that the terrorists are planning worldwide for the US. I have made ardent efforts to get this message out. That those hearing these messages need to know they are from me, Princess Diana, royal peace worker for Earth and its inhabitants. Do not fail me. Do not fail peace for this precious gem, Earth. We all salute and bow to you, royal peace workers like myself.

Press on the cause for peace, for your children, and your children's children, too, so that a New Age of peace may dawn.

My loving comfort, Diana, Princess of Peace

Make Peace a Priority for Your Children! March 9, 2002

M: Di, I'm here to continue your work.

D: That's great. Lets' get started then. I want you to know how highly regarded you are here by the many who can see what you are doing to help, that you are indeed loved and appreciated here, as well as by the many who are fortunate to know you in your world.

M: Lately it sure doesn't seem that way. I've been feeling so all alone in the world. Things not going well with my life, I guess.

D: That will soon change, as much in your world will soon change. Have faith in yourself.

Now, I wish to return to world affairs. This time in human history, we are seeing in spirit here that the murders and horrors that humans are inflicting upon themselves have to stop! The Middle Eastern area is a bloodbath, with no less than 55 deaths in one day, Palestinians and Israeli's combined! That if this can't be resolved, it will be a bloodbath worldwide for many who are not directly involved or responsible. **Again, I am urging the Allied Powers especially the US and Britain and their allies, to come to the Peace Table. There is no one who can do this for the world but you! And if you fail, it will mean more terror on US soil.** Therefore, the cease-fire, which must be negotiated first with the help of United Nations peacekeeping forces, and then the Accord which will draw up boundary lines for the state of Palestine will be negotiated. Mr. Zinni, Mr. Powell, Mr. Annan, and Mr. Blair could all be doing this now, before more terror breaks out on US soil! **The Middle East peace accord will do much to ease tensions in the Arab world setting the record straight, and liberating the Palestinian people, who have suffered enough!**

M: Diana, I was so glad to see they are catching on to the crisis, and sending Mr. Zinni, that there seems to be hope. Don't they realize what is at stake here? Do they think there is anyone else that can do the diplomatic work besides them? I ask these questions rhetorically.

D: It must be our leaders, who else can negotiate the peace. Certainly, Mr. Sharon and Mr. Arafat can be involved as things progress but they are not speaking at the moment. Certainly neither can call to order an Accord; there is too much hatred between them.

M: I was wondering about that. Yes, they seem to be archenemies. We need tactful negotiations, diplomats with grace and words of gentleness, as well as people who can strike a land deal for Palestine. Someone has to do this! It can't be postponed. Not one more bloody day of that!

D: Darling you're beginning to sound like me. We in spirit are tired of the senseless children's games that the human race is playing with the sacred gift of life. There are many coming over here the victims of senseless violence and murder, even children. Children should not have to face murder! Whether Israeli or Palestinian child, they are but children. Won't someone do something?

M: It's absolutely an outrage that children are being murdered in this. They're lawless over there.

D: I know that the aforementioned leaders are all well aware of the worsening situation. We wish to commend them for their brave acts in coming forth for the rights of so many oppressed people. And we wish to further add that if they can do this one thing, all will in time be right with the New World Order which will emerge from this, **whereby your world will literally transform from a battle ground where blood once was, to a lovely garden, where flowers grow, children play, and all are safe!** Humanity can do this for herself. She has the help of the Almighty Creator and those of us who guard over her now, from Heaven. Do this one thing: **Make peace a priority for your children, and your children's children, in the name of your God!**

This message is from Diana, Princess of Peace for your world. My love to all.

Be Harbingers of Peace March 14, 2002

M: Diana, it's me. If there is something you wish to say, I'm here.

D: Thank you Darling, you see you needn't worry so about the temporal things of life. You're being looked after here from spirit.

M: I'm indeed grateful, it's that the appearance of the layoff and the divorce at once seems like something ominous, as though I need to do something about it all.

D: Yes, this may be true in time, but right now there is urgent business pertinent to the world at large. I wish to speak.

M: By all means, have your say, Diana.

D: I wish to say that the Peace Accord that is being planned for cease-fire must not end there, or there will be more bloodshed. Instead, and in addition to the cease-fire, we wish to recommend that the negotiations begin for Palestine, for its boarders to be drawn up. We ask that Mr. Annan and the UN set up a peacekeeping force in Palestine/Israel, and that this be part of the agreement, that no diplomats leave the region before they have set up a peace keeping force for good there. It may need to be a semi-permanent arrangement, I am afraid to say. Needless to say, though, it will be very well thought out and necessary to prevent the bloodshed we have all seen in these last horrific weeks.

M: Di, do go on.

D: Additionally, if the boundary lines can be drawn up for Palestine, at least in theory, at some time they can then be ratified by the Palestinian Parliament and the Israeli Parliament so as to legalize the State of Palestine. This will be great cause for rejoicing for both sides, for the cause for a homeland can then be realized, and Israel can at last rest in peace every night. **I'm afraid to say that if this deal cannot be struck so much unnecessary bloodshed will then happen all over the world through further terrorist attacks, and on US soil! It must be clearly understood by the diplomats that this is what the real crisis is, Palestine, and this is what the terrorists want. Therefore give to them their demands, and be done with terror and terrorists, at least for the most part. They won't disappear but the reason for the terrorist groups fomenting in the first place will then be gone!**

M: You're brilliant, Diana!

D: Not really, not at all. We in spirit can view future outcomes. We watch movies of possible projections and make accurate predictions based on the projections. As I said, it's kind of like the CD ROM that most of you are familiar with. We enjoy a kind of TV here, too.

M: Wow, I had no idea really except what I read about in Michael's book, <u>The Stars Still Shine: An Afterlife Journey</u> (channeled by Robert Murray). Boy, was that some book, Di! What he described was a Heaven so real. Is it that real?

D: We're getting off track. Yes, heaven is real. And our experience is real, even though our bodies are more light than yours and we travel at a thoughts speed. That is how I am with you now; through thought. Now back to peacemaking. **I am again asking that the nations come to table, strike this deal for Palestine, so that there can be no confusion about it: The US and Britain are on the side of the underdog!** This will do much to ease tensions in the Arab World, right before the summit. It will fare much better than the other prospect of just a cease-fire. The Arab world is upset at the news leak about nuclear weapons, and has their own weapons of mass destruction, as I have repeatedly warned you about! Therefore tread carefully with those nations most feared. And be harbingers of peace to the war torn world at this sad moment in time. My love and consolation, Diana Princess of Peace.

An Exceptional Message, Through Robert Murray

A Confirmation of Princess Diana

In this interlude between channeling I wish to highlight a few extraordinary occurrences which happened to me in the last few months that further validate my work with Princess Diana.

Robert Murray, author of the Stars Still Shine: An Afterlife Journey, (www.TheStarsStillShine.com)[5] and channel for Michael (his deceased son in law) contacted me recently with a channeled message that confirmed, once again this was genuinely Princess Diana's voice I hear!

His book details Michael's experience of heaven, and Robert has also received some channeled messages from Princess Diana, because according to Michael, he ascended to a different level of heaven and now lives in a house next door to Princess Diana!

As I was reading this fascinating account of the afterlife, a couple of really interesting things happened. I had just finished the book when Robert received a channeled message from both Michael and Diana. Michael quoted Diana as saying that his little daughter, as well as his wife, came over to the other side in sleep and visited with Princess Diana at her home. This is an excerpt of the email I received from Robert Murray, in Diana's words, as paraphrased by Michael, when she then stepped in.

---

[5] Murray, Robert. *The Stars Still Shine: An Afterlife Journey.* Aura Publishing, Vermont, © 2002 www.TheStarsStillShine.com

"I have not forgotten you. I have you inked in to my agenda book. That is to say I have you inked in every day. Usually it reads 'Father Murray'. When I see your name it reminds me and I rush off to plant the news or at most times--direction into someone's ear. That is spelled with an 'e'. I am so very pleased that you have caught up with Marcia. I am afraid that I work her very hard and give her no rest. She is a dear and helps so much. God bless her, you and all your lovely family. Tell your Diana (referring to Diane who is James's mother and Father Murray's wife) that she has amazing patience and is loved by all. Of course I cannot leave out James. He is one of the most efficient people I have ever met. I would have certainly added him to my staff had I known him when I was in full body. I must be off to bother someone else. love and peace, Diana

Diana has a way of taking over. As I started to quote her she popped in and took over. It saved me a lot of time. Diana has left the building."

love and peace, Mike xxx ooo Lynn and Emily

Another Confirmation of Diana The Spiritualist Church

As if this weren't enough, in one month, I had another confirmation from another source, within the weeks that followed this awe inspiring message from Robert Murray! This really satisfied my mind that this really is the spirit of Princess Diana speaking almost daily to me.

Bob had recommended the Spiritualist church, and so had Jan, a friend of mine. They said that they do healings and readings there, and I might find company for my work. Well, I dragged my husband off to LeRoy, Illinois on what both of us thought of as a wild goose chase, not knowing if we'd even find the church. It was two hours away from home. When we got there we pulled into a gas station to ask directions. No one had heard of the Spiritualist Church, and this was a small town! But the man who I asked was kind enough to offer to drive us there, since he was a native to that town. (A moment of grace, no doubt!)

So we went wildly searching down more little streets, with the help of the stranger, until every last turn had been exhausted. I began to wonder if I'd find it, when I looked across the street to see the sign, "Spiritualist Church." So, after we came in and were seated, we realized they were into a healing service, and they were doing the laying on of hands. So we sat back and observed. Then we sang this hymn called "Beulah-land," a weird hymn about heaven! After hymns, they were preparing to do Greetings from Spirit. At that moment, I felt as if a bolt of lightning suddenly hit me, and I immediately straightened up. I felt a presence of something, it must have been Diana. They went around to everyone in the congregation, telling people what Spirit was showing them. That in itself was awesome.

The reader, Patrick, stopped when he came to me, and said this, "You are surrounded by Spirit. I see a nun in a blue and white habit, standing behind you. She is holding a baby, in a kind of blue light. Now, I don't know what this means, but I am just telling you what I see."

I said, "Thank you, and, would it possibly be Mother Teresa?"

Patrick replied, "Yes, that is who it is. Now this child maybe wants to reincarnate, and maybe she was one of Mother Teresa's nuns or something. And, oh, I see Diana standing behind you too. I used to do readings for Princess Diana in life, so I know it's her! I don't know what this all means, I am just telling you what I see in Spirit!"

I said "Thank you so much, Patrick. Can I talk to you after church about this?"

" Of course," Patrick replied. I had never met Patrick. Patrick had never met me.

Coincidence? No, it was not a coincidence. It was one of the most extraordinary experiences I have ever had. Even the man that appeared at the gas station seemed intent to help us find that church.

Later Patrick and some church members got together to hear me read excerpts from my new book, Princess Diana's Message of Peace, to discuss her presence in my life, and possibly to bring a message from her that night. They wanted a séance, which I wasn't at all used to nor was I interested, particularly. I have never been to a séance. I continued to read from my manuscript. I read some of Diana's earlier messages from September 11th and onward, to illustrate her knowledge of political global power. They were awed as I sat there reading. It was Patrick[6] who wanted to see Princess Diana materialize before his eyes. That didn't happen. I continued with my reading of Diana's messages. Everyone sat there so still, I believe they were awe struck! They invited me back to give a lecture there at the Spiritualist Church in LeRoy. That was my second confirmation of my work with Diana in the same month, (March, 2002), from what seemed out of nowhere! This church has always welcomed me, and the beautiful messages from the spirit of Princess Diana.

---

[6] Patrick James was the speaker and reader for the church service that day at the LeRoy (Crumbaugh) Spiritualist Church. Patrick James is a renowned medium and psychic, and he told me that day at church, that at one time, he owned a shop in London, and was a Psychic Reader for Princess Diana. He took a call from her when she was in crisis, and that is how the connection was made

Diana, Ambassador for Peace for Your World March 23, 2002

M: Hi, Di, it's me!

D: I'm so glad you called. It's been a while since we last spoke. I'm so glad that you found that special book you're holding in your hands now.

M: Oh, are you? Why? I know it has some old photos of you, and that it's the first edition of *Diana: Her True Story* by Andrew Morton.

D: To be perfectly honest, Morton was my only true biographer. The rest were flawed for one reason or another. I respected him, and his fine research. He didn't make things up, like the tabloids did. And he really went for what was genuine and dear to my heart. I'll always be grateful to Andrew and to you!

M: Di, I never thought you'd throw in a compliment like that for me! After all, you don't think Morton or any of his types read these books do you?

D: Indeed they do! You're both on par with my truth, my true spirit. You, now, with the fine peace work you are doing on my behalf, and Morton, for having laid the groundwork, so to speak!

M: So, I was supposed to go to town to find this book then?

D: Yes, but if not that way, it would find you another way. Now, on to peace work and the reason we came to dialogue. Commence the Peace Accord, you Nations! If I had a theme song, a title for these communications now, that would be it.

M: Maybe you need Michael, your friend who lives next door to you now!

D: Yes, he has done some marvelous things for us here, to bring causes to our awareness. Michael is absolutely a God send. But what this world needs is the Peace Accord. You met the Palestinian woman at the restaurant. You spoke your words to her. **This is what all Palestinians need to hear: that their cause for a homeland is just. If Israel is sincere in wanting peace, they must be willing to give up lands aquisitioned since the 1967 War, and be willing to draw up boundary lines. That this important part of the Peace Accord must not be ignored, for the consequences will be dire if it is.**

There will be more and more terror, and possible outright war between Israel and Palestine, if she (the state of Palestine) is not acknowledged by the powerful nations.

M: Diana, you're always one step ahead. We've all been praying for peace, I am keen to your insistence that this state of Palestine be created soon. I just wonder though, can Peacekeepers be sent in? And are we doing enough?

D: The United States is definitely on the offensive with another agenda, that of Iraq, but equally they realize and are negotiating for a cease-fire in the region. And they are now well aware of the seriousness of the needs of the Palestinian people for a state, a homeland. They are working towards this goal. At the same time, it is getting harder to get the sides to meet, since the violence is growing, the malice between the states is growing, and it's becoming harder to adopt a Palestinian state when so much of the violence is being taught and employed within their ranks, particularly the suicide bombers, who are wreaking so much havoc. Mr. Arafat has condemned their actions and does not stand for this terror, but they are defying his orders and doing it anyway, so desperate is their cry for help.

M: Are you saying then, Di, that their actions are a cry for help, as it says in *A Course in Miracles*,[7] "...all attack is a cry for help"?

D: That is precisely what they are crying about. They don't care if they die, thinking they are going to heaven, doing good for Allah. It's truly sad, because this is not the will of Allah, and does not gain them anything, but further sets them back, here in the afterlife. And it certainly does no good in the present life, for all the murder they are creating is so sad really. They need to understand, here and now, that they are weakening Mr. Arafat's cause for a homeland, and to stop it immediately!

---

[7] Foundation for Inner Peace. A Course in Miracles, Text. ©.1985 Tiboron CA, used with permission

M: That was stronger than I've ever heard you speak Diana. You must hate seeing so many innocent lives given up for such a stupid reason! I wish they'd be able to see your words, Di.

Maybe they'd listen to an international figure such as you.

D: Thank you for your kind words. I am emphatic that if the Peace Accord goes on, that the suicide bombers stop their hideous game of evil; for their own good and that of their children.

M: Thank you, Diana, Ambassador for Peace in the Middle East. You have my vote. Is there anything else?

D: I am closing shortly. I wish to thank again those diplomats most closely involved with the peace making process, wherever they may be. That they are to be commended for their persistence, and I ask that they continue to court Mr. Arafat, and not to blame him for the terrorists gone out of control and that these members of the various groups are inciting them to do this. I ask all to pray for Peace in the Middle East, and for all to continue to try to come to table, and create the Palestinian State, so that there can be no mistaking it in the minds of the Arab world: the US is on the side of the underdog, and stands for justice for all. My love to all at this critical juncture, Diana, Ambassador for Peace for your world.

My Heartfelt Sympathy for Netanya March 28, 2002

M: Diana, it's me. I'm wondering what your thoughts are on the evolving situation in the Mid East?

D: I thought you'd never call. I am very deeply saddened by the increasing violence on the part of the suicide bomber, especially in Netanya yesterday. It was deeply distressing, and we express our heartfelt sympathy for those who lost loved ones.

M: Yes, I was horrified at that and wondered if the Palestinian cause would go on with that much carnage and bloodshed, done at the Seder meal. It's such a sacrilege, Di!

D: You are quite correct on that point, but if the Israeli's really want peace, here is their chance. They must rise above the need for vengeance for yesterday's actions. They themselves know in their law that an eye for an eye, a tooth for a tooth doesn't work. As deeply grievous as this latest action was, it again confirms the necessity of the Peace Accord. I so strongly urge our diplomats not to give in to jargon in both sides of the issue but to remain steadfast in the Peace process. Take Mr. Arafat to his word! Go with his word to the peace table! Do not let this act of violence intimidate you!

It must be obvious to leaders that Mr. Arafat has no real power to harness some of the perpetrators of yesterday's crimes. His hands are tied by the Israeli government. Therefore it is quite hypocritical if not impossible to hold him accountable for a criminal act that he had nothing to do with!

M: Di, today is Holy Thursday. Couldn't we see them at table, putting an end to senseless evils like this. It's really very sad that they feel they must use violence to achieve their aim, but in a way I think it is making Israel think about the consequences of the outright oppression of the Palestinian people. At the same time, this kind of murder is totally unjustified.

D: Part of the difficulty of Israel coming to peace has to do with the Sharon government. In that Mr. Arafat and Mr. Sharon are long standing enemies, and this is playing into the stalemate with negotiations. I commend so highly the noble Peace Plan put forth by Crown Prince Abdullah, of Saudi Arabia. It's a brilliant plan, and one that ought to be put into place, as well as the Tenet plan.

M: Diana, I'm not sure what the exact conditions of the plans are, but could you perhaps be more specific?

D: Well, the Tenet plan is more conservative than the one conceived by Prince Abdullah. While the specifics are different it doesn't really matter until the US gets Israel in the peace process, it's going to be drawn out. I'm calling upon our US diplomats to continue in their ardent efforts not to lose hope or to give in to the pressures from either side. Pursue the peace process, and don't leave the area until the deal is signed in ink!

M: Di, is there anything else?

D: Our thoughts and prayers are with you, especially all of the diplomats involved in brokering peace in the shattered remains of the latest carnage in Israel. **Our sympathies are with those families and with all involved; we ask that this ridiculous carnage come to an immediate end!** Mr. Arafat is right in calling an immediate end to the violence, and we in spirit ask that all pray for peace for the entire region, for the world is hanging on this thread of hope for peace right now. We must stop all violence in the name of religious hatred! My love and prayers are with this peace process. Do not give up, all my loving consolation in a troubled time, Diana, Princess of Peace.

Diana's Easter Message of Peace God Speed to the Americans! April 1, 2002

M: Di, I've been awake, thinking something you might say might save the situation in Israel.

D: Thanks for calling, It' so very thoughtful of you. We are working on a solution to the crisis as we speak. We haven't worked out the details as of yet, so we wish to discuss them more at length and get back to you in the morning. We know what you know, and more, you needn't feel so personally responsible.

M: It's the thought of saving a life; an Israeli or a Palestinian might be saved, or Mr. Arafat or Mr. Sharon's life for that matter. I can't sleep thinking you have the answers, Di.

D: Well, we'll see you bright and early, I do have answers, and you'll be ready to hear them then. Sleep well, Darling.

M: Di, it's me. I'm ready to hear from you!

D: That's great Darling, we'll get going on it now. The situation in the Middle East calls for intervention. In this sad scenario, neither side is winning the war against terror. Mr. Arafat is holed up fighting for his life and that of his men. He does not believe that the Israeli's will let him live in peace there, and will attempt to capture him. This situation that has arisen after capturing his compound is in fact worsening the crisis over there with regard to suicide bombers. You see, the Palestinian people feel that terror is now their only weapon against Israel who has in fact declared war upon them. How can they defend themselves? While it is true that the suicide bombings, particularly on the Passover in Netanya caused all this, Mr. Arafat can do little to nothing in his present circumstances to control the terrorist factions. I must repeat again: Mr. Arafat does not sanction terror, nor stand for it! He is not the author of these bombings nor does he give orders for it. He is however becoming exhausted and confused in his compound, without support from any country, and needs help to do the job he is required to do, clean up the terrorists! Furthermore, Mr. Sharon is clearly not handling the situation in a productive way. Steps need to be implemented for a cease-fire right away, and this is where

US intervention is crucial to the peace process.

M: Di, I think and most diplomats from other presidencies (CNN aired a special last night on the history of the Palestinian conflict with Israel) agree that diplomacy is the answer to this delicate problem. If the US isn't willing or able to go in and rescue Mr. Arafat, help him save face and round up terrorists, then who will? Are we to let the bloodletting continue, let the Palestinians continue to act out their rage against the innocent Israeli people? That is precisely how they are reacting to the recent military strike against them: with more terror. Mr. Arafat is going to fall, and who will replace him? Do you have any recommendations on how the situation might be solved? And also, Mr. Sharon is a military person, and is under indictment for war crimes in the Hague, for having ordered the mass killing of innocent Palestinians. He seems too military to be diplomatic in this: he is reliving the good old days of battle. Here we have two military personalities pitted against each other. It is truly a no-win situation.

D: Let it be clear that the role of the US is to send further diplomats into the region. That this can be the top guns if they choose, because Israel isn't listening to anyone in the UN or the US (who is not someone of importance). If someone high ranking were to meet with Arafat, it would lend support to the cause for a homeland. If not, the situation will simply deteriorate into outright war in the entire region. But we caution: if this is so, then don't waste the energy: go with a definite plan of action. Ask for help from a UN peacekeeping force if they are willing. Invite Mr. Arafat (or an envoy) to a neutral country, and a top ranking Israeli official, not Mr. Sharon. In this way, the parties will be more cooperative. Perhaps a cease-fire can be obtained. **If not, I am afraid to say what I am seeing in spirit. The Arab countries (in alliance with Palestine) will be pitted against the US and Israel, and more and more terrorist attacks will riddle the region. The US will likely be a target of terror again and again, both abroad and at home.**

I so wish to say that the US has everything to gain from intervention of some sort, and that the diplomats should have a plan of action before they go to the region. I wish God speed to the Americans on this diplomatic endeavor should they choose to do this!

In this way and only in this way will the war on terror be won: by addressing the needs of the underdog, (Palestine) in such a way that justice is done for a lesser country, and to bring peace to the region! We in spirit salute all the peace workers including those from America and Europe who stand beside Mr. Arafat in his compound at this time. All My love and compassion, Diana, Princess of Peace.

God Speed, Mr. Powell! April 6, 2002

M: Di, I'm here to be your voice today. I am listening.

D: Thank you dearest, we are so grateful for your continued effort in these messages. You've no idea how important they really are! They are indeed reaching those diplomats we've pointed out to you through the inter net, so by whatever means possible, don't give up! We salute and bow to all the royalty who are doing this peace work at this crucial time!

M: Aren't you delighted to see Mr. Colin Powell going on a mission of peace to the Mid-East?

D: We indeed are totally delighted, pleased and commend his bravery and integrity in standing up to the increasing incursions in Palestine. While at the same time, we regret that Israel is making life so difficult for so many innocent people in the Palestinian refugee camps and cities. We hope that a just solution can be reached for both sides, Israel as well. For it is not without reason that they have launched this offensive against the Palestinian people. We hope to see a cease-fire and a deal for a Palestinian homeland struck with his mission.

M: Diana, that is a tall order. You know that the leadership with Palestine and Israel is in opposition; that Sharon and Arafat are archenemies. What can you recommend or what should be done to lessen that, get around it?

D: Well, it's all over your news. New leaders are being sought out as we speak. And in this, I wish to say that the leadership within the Palestinian State must come from within their ranks, or it will be disregarded. While Mr. Colin Powell is taking steps to meet with Arab leaders on this very issue, it will not work unless Palestine is directly involved in that leadership.

M: The Palestinian spokesman who was featured on CNN this morning, Saeb Erakat, seems like a very reasonable man, perhaps he could be dealt with as a spokesman who may engage the peace process with other Israeli representatives other than Sharon, and of course Mr. Zinni.

D: All the diplomacy will work if the sides are able to agree. It is a delicate matter. If in addition to the cease- fire, the arrangements for a Palestinian state could be mandated, with a peace keeping force as well, it stands a very good chance. This may involve months of negotiations, some of which will be behind the scenes. We commend the United States for showing its integrity and courage not to let Israel totally destroy the Palestinian people.

M: There's a lot of press about Britain right now, with the death of the boys great-grandmother, the Queen Mum, and then Prime Minister Blair's visit, is there anything you wish to say on the subject of either? We're sad to see the boys behind another funeral procession.

D: I want my boys to know how much I love them, and I express my sympathy for the loss of the Queen Mum. She was a dear person, whom I was glad to have known. Her contributions were well known throughout the bombing of

London, and she will be remembered for her courage. We wish to further add that she is in good company here in Heaven, and is being looked after!

As for the alliance with Mr. Blair and Mr. Bush, we commend that further talks are underway for the creation of a Palestinian State, and further discussion about terror in the Middle East. All will succeed with the meeting this weekend. What remains to be seen is the incursion in Israel/Palestine, and whether that will stop soon. We ask further prayers for a cease-fire in the region and a total pullout of Israeli troops from Palestinian areas, as soon as possible.

I again commend the United States and Mr. Powell for his remarkable courage in preventing further catastrophe in the region. We wish to say that while it will be a very difficult agenda, all of heaven is with him on this important mission and we wish him God Speed!

My love and compassion at this time, Diana,

Ambassador for Peace for your world

Diana, Peacemaker, © 2002, watercolor, Marcia McMahon.

11. In this lovely portrait of Diana, (previous page) we see her in her evolving role as a Peacemaker for Earth. She was visiting Bosnia, in 1997, listening to the war torn people and offering hope and consolation. This was part of her World Wide Alert to Land mines, and her last political trip, sometime in August 1997, shortly before she died. She was known to have listened to every person she could there, to send money and letters to the suffering people, offering the only source of hope to some. Diana would even ask if there was food in the home and have food delivered to those wounded by land mines in this region.

In this sense it isn't hard to conceive that Diana is speaking from heaven to assist all of us on Earth to bring forth peace before it is too late. To view this painting in color, go to:

ww.angelfire.com/mb2/diana_speaks/ and then go to Diana Gallery II.

All My Love to the Peacemakers! April 12, 2002

M: Di, I'm here for you if you need to say anything. I am listening.

D: You're most dear to be open to my voice at this time. This past week has seen unparalleled violence in the Mid East, and we are sorry to see the setback today with another suicide bomber in Jerusalem.

M: It was certainly a setback. I might add though, that the Palestinians say their death toll is much higher, some five hundred or more people killed in major cities in the West Bank, in Nablus.

D: The death toll on both sides is perilous and mounting. Something must be done to curb the continued violence. I am afraid to say that the mission Mr. Powell is on has been deterred by the Israelis and their rhetoric, while at the same time the Palestinians are being murdered en-mass in their cities. Mr. Arafat feels he can't condemn the suicide bombings now, though he has in the past, because he feels that his people have a right to defend themselves in the bloody onslaught of tanks, artillery and rounding up of innocent civilians. There is murder going on in those camps and that is why the news authorities aren't allowed into the refugee camps! It is a bloodbath in some of them!

In this message I am trying to stand up for the innocent lives on both sides, but I must say that Mr. Powell is getting only one side as he sits with the Israeli heads of state. That to be fair and broker peace he must be open to hear the concerns of Mr. Arafat, even though there was another suicide bombing.

M: On that point, can you comment on the documents that were confiscated this week that supposedly confirm Mr. Arafat's signature for payment for suicide bombers to their families? I would never say that you said anything untrue but this is what they found.

You have repeatedly claimed that Mr. Arafat is a dove, and doesn't condone this violence. I apologize for putting you on the spot, if you can shed light on this matter please do.

D: I will say this much: it is news to all of us! We in spirit see no direct connection of Mr. Arafat to these documents or to the suicide bombers. We do see that there are extremist Palestinian terror organizations who claim to be with Mr. Arafat's Fatah movement, but they are not authorized by him personally to do these acts of horror. We cannot further comment because we don't have further information.

M: And again I apologize for sounding as if I might be doubting your wonderful words. I trust you completely and have never questioned your integrity or honesty, Di. It was a question of who was behind these things at all. Thank you for your light, to all of us at this time. We all love you and your courage for intervening in human affairs on behalf of the world.

D: On a more personal note, I was thrilled to see your work with the children this morning, and the crowns you all made! That was a very special moment to me, and thank you for keeping my memory alive. The children all love you and you will be missed when you go from there.

M: I'm so pleased to speak of you to children everywhere. They all love you, Diana. Of course I can tell them I'm writing a book about you, but I can't tell them it's channeled by you! That would be overwhelming to them. But in time they will see your picture on the cover and then they'll know.

D: Back to business at hand. We in spirit salute and bow to the royalty doing this peace work and ask Mr. Colin Powell not to give up his mission. That we have said it would be difficult and seem impossible, heartbreaking though it is to see this terrible violence. He will in time be able to broker a cease-fire, perhaps with the aid of Mr. Annan of the UN, and bring in the Peacekeepers. That persistence will pay off very big for the world and especially the United States if he can persist in the face of apparent failure and ridicule even amongst his own cabinet members who may disagree and want to send him home. The road to peace is paved by those with vision. **He is just such a man, and this will take him to new heights personally and politically if he should choose this endeavor. The heavenly host surround him and no physical harm will come to him as well. We watch over him with great care, asking of course that he do his own will as we respect his right to do.[8] All my love to him and all peace workers, Diana, Princess of Peace.**

---

[8] This channeled message was delivered Friday, the same day there was another suicide bombing in Jerusalem, hitting very close to where peace negotiations were going on. Colin Powell was debating on not seeing Mr. Arafat at all after this.

Diana makes it clear here that it was important to see Arafat and hear his concerns. Later, Saturday, Mr. Powell did decide to go into the besieged compound and pay a visit on Mr. Arafat. Perhaps Mr. Powell has an angel (Diana) on his shoulder!

Dawn of the New Age for Arab, Christian and Jew April 19, 2002

M: Di, I am here for you, and won't fail you, if there is anything you wish to say.

D: Darling, thank you and know you are indeed appreciated. We know you are tired from your week but we are grateful to hear from you. I will shortly comment on Colin Powell's peace mission and its aftereffects.

M: I found it rather heartbreaking for both sides, that nothing was accomplished in either a cease-fire or an end to the incursions. It did not appear that they have any better handle on Mr. Arafat's situation either.

D: It is best not to judge apparent failure. For you yourself know that all failure leads to eventual success if one is determined enough. Obviously, the tensions and fighting was too fierce with the Israeli incursions to do much good. Mr. Powell was trying to get both sides to cease-fire, and both were busy blaming the other party. As long as that kind of thinking persists they will remain in a stalemate. What Mr. Powell and the Administration are now working toward is something unique that may help both to come to terms much easier. They are drafting the boundary lines of the Palestinian State with the help of all countries, and plan to invite the Arab states into the bargain as well. It is quite a good idea really, and will succeed if they persist in effort.

M: Isn't there anything you'd recommend in the interim process to ease the suffering there? I am feeling that it's so very hopeless for the Palestinians, and obviously dangerous for the Jews in the region too.

D: The attempt to mediate a deal failed largely because Mr. Sharon failed to withdraw his troops in a timely fashion. Had he done that, Mr. Arafat might have been amenable to the demands placed upon him for a variety of things. The concessions they were demanding seemed so overwhelming since he is still under siege.

M: Yes, now as I understand it, they want the men he is holding for the assassination of the Israeli cabinet minister in the compound, and they want a total cessation of suicide bombings.

D: That is correct. And they are asking this of someone who clearly isn't in control of his people because his resources have been cut off. He doesn't have the means to communicate effectively with his people in order to command them. It is very sad really that the civilized governments of the world are treating him this way and asking him to come up with all the right answers. He is isolated and cut off from most forms of communication!

M: My feelings are the same. It seems a cruel situation, but one that perhaps Mr. Arafat may have inadvertently allowed to happen for failing to curtail his own countrymen from all those horrible suicide bombers.

D: Indeed, all of this was not under his control. But on a lighter note I wish to say that the current ideas being explored are all worth the effort. If we can bring peace to the region, it will likely bring the promised 1,000 years of peace, eventually for all the world. Therefore, do not be distressed by apparent failure. **Persist and don't give up the process of dialogue and peacemaking!** It will do much to restore world order, and faith in the United States in particular when much of the Arab world is quite faithless. **My brothers and sisters in faith, I ask you all not to give up hope on one another, Arab, Jew or Christian. For in time, God willing, you shall have your promised land. Not just Palestine, but the promised years of peace and the dawning of the New Age!** For Arab, Jew and Christian can learn to appreciate differences and live in harmony and peace.

My love and compassion, Diana,
Ambassador for Peace for your world

Stop the Violence in the Name of God! April 27, 2002

M: Di, I am here to listen to your voice. Is there anything you wish to say?

D: Hello, Darling, I am now listening as well. We have been waiting to comment on the current world affairs issues. We thank you for your contact.

M: Well, I see President Bush met with Crown Prince Abdullah this week, and I was pleased to see that happen.

D: Indeed we were thrilled! We are very happy that they met and discussed further prospects for peace in the Mid East, which is what we're all hoping for at this time. The Peace Plan that the Crown Prince set forth will work, if the Administration will give in to some of the demands upon Israel. And there are differences in the opinion on the Peacekeepers in the region. The US is reluctant to commit Peacekeepers due to security concerns. But I wish to say that all would be well with them there to safeguard both Israel and Palestine. To prevent what happened just today, in Israel, for instance. A Palestinian militant crept into an Israeli occupied settlement and killed quite a few civilians. With the Peacekeepers at hand, it is unlikely that this would happen as often. As to whether Israel is willing to give on certain issues, such as the Jewish Settlements, will also be a bartering point in negotiations. We encourage her to do so, in order to create peace. Giving up a bit of land is a small price to pay for world peace. For in restoring the state of Palestine to the world, world peace can be bought, at a price, albeit a high one for Israel. Just what is a human life worth?

And should not the lives of both sides be worth more than a parcel of land here and there? Therefore, my brothers and sisters who want peace: **Learn to accept differences and be willing to bargain, for you can only gain for all the world in this bargain! Accept the plan of God that He would have you have: peace, prosperity, and the continuation of the human race!** For indeed, the other scenario is just as likely, and indeed very, very grim: that of continued violence and war, and possible World War, I might add!

M: I know, Di, that the reason you're sending messages now is to prevent the later scenario. I am most grateful to be a messenger for you. And the world at large seems to be in agreement that Palestine must exist alongside Israel for any lasting peace in the region.

D: Correct, and we feel that will solve much of the world terror, and the terror in the region. While there is no real death, as is evidenced in my words now, we wish to see fewer people passing into spirit due to the continued violence. **We wish to see Heaven on Earth, and the dawning of the New Age, whereby mankind can expand his/her God given abilities, such as what you are tapping into now in your channeled messages.** There is far more than meets the eye in personal development and spirituality now dawning. If the leaders of the world will listen to reason, to one another, and put petty land disputes and religious differences aside, and learn to walk amongst themselves as brothers! This has been my plea since the beginning of my messages with you! And still we see such terrible deeds and hatreds! This is the time for the human race to be born anew, to stop the hatred, the aggression, the violence especially in the name of God, who wills no violence upon innocent people. This message is being sent to you from Diana, the Peacemaker and Ambassador for Peace for your world. **My love to all, and especially the Peacemakers, who are the true royalty at this time!**

May Gardens Replace Graveyards! May 4, 2002

M: Di, it's me, I 'm here to hear your voice.

D: That's great Darling! We have much to comment on today, and we're always glad to hear from you. We know that you're tired, and still working so hard. Make time today to rest in the beautiful garden you're so hard at work in! I'll shortly begin my commentary on world affairs.

M: I will try to rest in it. It seems I can't stop working today!

D: That's quite all right, for without your hard work and concerted effort these messages wouldn't be getting out to those who need to hear them.

M: Is there anything you wish to comment on Di?

D: Yes, of course there is always an agenda. Though these conversations are by no means planned, they are truly conversations, and flow with you and your thoughts as well as mine and those who are with me in spirit. Now that you are centering in, you will find it easier to hear my voice through your thoughts. We in spirit commend the actions of all the peace workers worldwide. We were very pleased to see the release of Mr. Arafat from his compound in Ramallah. This is a helpful step towards peace. We are concerned that there has been no investigation into the massacre in Jenin, and likewise we are concerned now that tanks are entering Nablus, one of the larger West Bank towns.

We wish to emphasize that the Palestinian people have rights, which are being violated with these continued incursions, and we, like many throughout the world, want a stop to them. **Likewise it is our sincere hope that Mr. Arafat will again call upon his people to stop the suicide bombings altogether, and insist on integrity from his people! That will likewise help to create the longed for cease-fire and the longed for state of Palestine! A** world without war and terror is something that all the world's children are entitled to. It is for them that we are doing this, to create a future for your children, and your children's children! It is so important to have everyone understand the essential element of peace: that of forgiveness, and that without forgiveness of enemies, there will still be war.

M: Diana, those are beautiful words and thoughts, and I love children and want the same thing for them. A world without war is something every human being is entitled to, not just children, but they are of course more innocent and loving!

D: Your insight is so correct and you are a person after my own heart! The children of the world deserve our most concerted efforts so that they will not see bombs blowing up their fathers or mothers or brothers or sisters. That peace will become the norm, instead of this conflict.

M: Di, is there anything else you wish to comment on at this time?

D: I am closing shortly. We wish to see an end to the standoff at the Church of the Nativity. That it is the most holy site in all of Christendom, and revered throughout the world.

That it is full of symbolism, as it truly is the birthplace of Jesus the Christ. And the birth of Christ was threatened then, as it is now, by hatreds, religious intolerance and violence that needn't be! Whether you accept Jesus as your Savior or not, the church should not have been set ablaze! We are asking all the worlds diplomats in Israel, Palestine, and the US not to give up negotiations until this important landmark is saved.

And the birth of Christ within each heart is once again revered, as it should rightly be! For the Christ is the divine spark within each one of you, whether Christian, Muslim or Jew, and you needn't believe in Jesus to know that Christ within![9] **If mankind can navigate the twisted roads out of hatred and blame, there is much to be gained for all the world: a place where flowers grow, and gardens replace graveyards to those fallen in battle! Do this for the children, and the children's children! My love to all,**

Diana, Princess of Peace.

---

[9] Diana, once again urges the putting aside of religious differences. When she speaks of the Christ within, she is apparently speaking of the God-spark within each of us. For those truly seeking further clarification, may I suggest to you _A Course in Miracles,_ Text, " The Christ in You", Chapter 24, The Goal of Specialness: V. The Christ in You, p. 509, Copyright,1985 The Foundation for Inner Peace, Tiboron , CA (permission granted by Foundation for Inner Peace, now out of print) ACIM is now published by Viking, Penguin Books, Ltd, Harmondsworth, Middlesex, England

Diana's Message of Peace May 8, 2002

M: Di, it's me, I am hear to listen to your voice, and be your voice if there is anything you wish to say.

D: We're glad to hear from you and know how appreciated you are at this crucial juncture!

We wish to comment on today's world affairs. We are deeply saddened to see another suicide bombing, (suburb of Tel Aviv, billiards club) as we, like you on Earth were hopeful for an end to that useless violence!

M: Di, I am hoping that they don't send in more Israeli troops in another incursion. I know Sharon flew home early to meet with his cabinet.

D: We see that he is meeting now with his cabinet, and we wish to discourage another incursion into the West Bank or Gaza. There has been so much bloodshed already, and it's time for all this none sense to end! More spilling of human blood is not going to solve the problem!

M: Well, Di, forgive the rhetorical question, but what is going to solve the problem?

D: The Peacekeepers! Mr. Arafat has rightly called for help from the UN and the US to bring the Peacekeepers. It has long been our belief that this would work as a viable alternative to more incursions. Mr. Sharon will alienate himself from the Western world and EU if he continues his path of bloodshed in the occupied territories.

It must be perfectly apparent that there are right wing extremists in the Palestinian movements who are not under Mr. Arafat's control, who must be dealt with with a Palestinian police force as well. Mr. Arafat would have greater ability to control his people, and more intelligence capability as well, to have the unified police force Mr. Bush recommended yesterday. I am asking that Mr. Arafat continue in his office and that the unified force be given him, as well as the Peacekeepers as a means of controlling the extremist groups who are perpetrating these horrible deeds. It is so important that we not loose more human life, Palestinian or Israeli!

M: What about the talk of deposing Arafat? So many US and Israeli heads want that. Is that logical and sound advice?

D: I am cautioning against that. It would not be popular amongst the Palestinians, who elected him. And it might incite more violence, and add to their feelings of helplessness. It is best to keep Arafat in office, whether you personally like him or not.

M: Thank you for your comments Diana, I will send them on as requested.

D: That is indeed our wish that this be sent on directly as directed. And we are most grateful for your time and talent in listening to my voice. For it is with my voice that we can navigate a peaceful settlement to the Middle East and avert further terror for most civilians. This is our aim in spirit, whilst we can't do it for you, we are here when you call on us for help. For all of heaven is here for Earth at this crucial and sad time.

We wish there weren't so many roadblocks to peace. We also ask those who are inclined to pray or meditate for peace for the Mid East at this time. My love to all,

Diana,

Princess of Peace

Obstacles to Peace May 18, 2002

M: Di, I'm sorry it took so long for me to find time today, but here I am for you.

D: That's great Darling, and we aren't upset that there have been so many seeming obstacles to peace in your private life and affairs. We are very patient, as we have all eternity. It is mankind that doesn't have the time on his/her side. We shall shortly comment on world affairs.

M: I was so pleased that no real incursion occurred in Gaza after the leaks to the press about one.

D: Many are very tired of war there. They are beginning to count the death toll, and even Israeli soldiers didn't want to put themselves at risk when the people of Gaza had mine fields waiting for them! We ask a return to the peace table. We wish to see it sooner than later. Many reforms are being considered at this juncture, and we commend that the US is helping with that in terms of influence only. We see that a new leader for Palestine would emerge if elections were held, and that Mr. Arafat could continue on in service in some way as well.

M: I am wondering what they can do to get peace back on track? It has been a while since Secretary Powell's visit, and I am sure he wants something done soon.

D: This summer's summit on peace is an excellent initiative, which will bring in Arab states as well.

And the many recommendations of Prince Abdullah, Mr. Tenent, Mr. Powell and others will set the stage for a fusion of both Western and Eastern ideas which will all help the creation of the state of Palestine. But we caution you further, that while this is going on, there will still be radical extremists who will try and upset the peace process once more, that they are trying to thwart the process, and should be ignored. And the Israeli Cabinet is very conservative and neither they nor the Islamic extremists want peace. These are the obstacles to peace, and there must be clear cut objectives to get around them.

M: That all makes sense, Diana. We have seen suicide bombers every time there are major figures at the peace talks. I assume you mean more of that.

D: Indeed the stakes are high for all involved, and it is imperative to go on right through the continued terror or there will be no end in sight. We see a very good outcome for the Summer Summit, and ask that all involved do everything in their power to see this through, the creation of the state of Palestine! It will do so much to avert world terror!

M: Is that all for today?

D: Yes, Darling, I am closing shortly. We commend the efforts of all the peace workers now, both international figures and people behind the scenes, just like yourself who contribute time, talent and energy without reward of any kind. We bow to all the royalty at this time who are the peace workers and ask their prayerful support and action continue. My love to all,

Diana, Peace Worker and Princess of Peace

The Terror Alerts: Futher Warning to Americans May 25, 2002

M: Hi, Diana, it's me. I am here for you if there is anything you wish to say!

D: Darling, you're so tired. I am wondering if you ought to rest this evening and channel in the morning? We are indeed happy to hear from you and know how hard you've been working all day.

M: Diana, there are so many world issues right now, and I am here. Tomorrow there are other things as well. So, if there is anything for tonight, please let me know.

D: We wish to say that you are better off resting and letting your mind settle a bit before channeling. We wish you a restful evening and ask you not to worry so about the future, or about your trip. We see a happy outcome there with your family!

M: Thanks, Di, that's great. I'll get back to you.

M: Di, it's me. I'm feeling better and am here to listen to your voice.

D: That's great Darling. We have been waiting to comment on world affairs, as there is much that needs our mutual attentions right now. We are pleased to hear you're feeling better.

M: Well, Colin Powell just made a remarkable press conference in Russia and it's all about the Nuclear Arms reduction treaty there.

D: I'm so pleased to see Russia and the US in agreement on arms reduction. That is so important as increasing threats from terror threaten the world at large to have the two major superpowers in agreement on so many issues. The alliance will build and prove invaluable on the war on terror.

As increasing tensions mount in Pakistan and India, the US will want to provide guidance and diplomacy to further reduce the outbreak of war. Secretary Powell and others are well aware of this as a nuclear threat and are working with President Musharev on this very issue.

M: I want to ask you, Diana, is there anything to the recent threats of terror on US soil? You always and have repeatedly warned of more threats at home.

D: Thank you for asking. Yes, the answer is of course yes. **Since the beginning of my correspondence with you and the many reading these messages, there are specific concerns. I have repeated my warnings, that American soil will likely see some form of terror! I have warned also of the airplanes, for that is where they wish to strike. The weapons of mass destruction are being planned to be used as we speak!** There are all kinds of plots, some of which are known to your US intelligence. Vigilance and top security are urged. Some have already infiltrated your country, and other Arabs are on their way. Be especially careful on the holiday weekend, especially in New York and California. They have many plots, some which we have heard of, others which are known only to them.

M: Diana, on the point of the weapons of mass destruction, can you be more specific? I know you said in your earlier messages that they wanted to use them from the hijacked airplanes. Is this still a threat?

D: Indeed it is! **That if each airline would arm themselves or have the stun guns aboard, so much harm can be averted!** Whilst all the spin on the news has to do with homeland terror alerts, I wish to say that America must not let go any opportunity for peacemaking in the Middle East. This past week has seen again more suicide bombings, and that this activity must stop! If there is ever to be a Peace Accord and a Palestine [state], this barbaric activity must be stopped! If the Peacekeepers can be sent into the region it would do so much to prevent the suicide bombers! If the UN and the US can negotiate a deal for them it would help deter terror in the region until the Summer Summit can be held. **We in spirit see a very positive outcome for the Summer Peace Summit and want this for Earth at this time. We see it as a possible solution to worldwide terror to have the state of Palestine. For this is what much of the terror is all about, the rights of the underdog, Palestine.**

I urge all diplomats hearing these messages to not give up the cause for peaceful negotiation for Palestine, for this will solve much of the world terror now plaguing so many countries. **We ask a special blessing on America at this time, for it is indeed a great nation, under God, and we pray for peace and protection for all Americans who are under threat at this time. That this message is from Diana, the Peacemaker and Princess of Peace. My love to all at this time,**

Diana.

Do Not Fail the Children of Earth! June 1, 2002

M: Di, it's me. I'm here for you now, to listen to your voice.

D: That's great, Darling. We'll get started now. There is much that needs our mutual attentions today.

M: Is there anything you wish to address?

D: I'm getting started shortly. While it is indeed commendable that diplomats are working round the clock to prevent the outbreak of war, nuclear war, I am afraid to say what I'm seeing in spirit!

M: Oh, my God, no, Diana! What are you seeing?

D: Darling take heart, it is just a possibility of loss of so much life in India and Pakistan! We warn their leaders, President Musharraf and others not to resort to this, for the devastation would be total, and we further add that all of humanity would be affected, so much so that the aftereffects of radiation would poison the planet!

M: They've got to resolve the issue of Kashmir in a practical way. Have you any suggestions, Di?

D: First and foremost, Kashmir has long been a source of contention in the region. Diplomacy, artful diplomacy, with the division of Kashmir and the cessation of gunfire on both sides would be a beginning. We wish to see all world leaders intervene in this crisis. It can be done but time is of the essence here. We also see the unfortunate consequences to the porous border of northern Pakistan with regard to the war on terror there. I have repeatedly warned that Muslim extremists would attempt to divert the attentions of Pakistan by starting trouble elsewhere in Pakistan, and this is just what they want: another war!

Mr. Musharraf is correct in rooting out all Muslim extremists in his country, and those who teach this perversion of Islam in their Mosques. For the entire region needs spiritual reeducation! **Dodi wishes to say that this extremism is a perversion of the truth of Islam, and that no one should listen to this. That this killing in the name of Allah is not what Mohammed intended! His wish is for Muslims in the region to live in peace with other brethren of different faith persuasions, and not to resort to crimes of bloodshed over religious differences.**

M: Di, I've heard this before and I want to say thank you to Dodi again for standing on his principles. I was so delighted on a personal note, to find the pictures from your day, the funeral, and see the many tributes to you and Dodi.

D: Indeed, so much of the sentiments were so true and from the heart. I thank everyone for their expressions of love and flowers! In closing then, I wish to commend the efforts of the diplomats, who are the true royalty at this time, and all the peacemakers everywhere, especially in the Middle East, that we are most grateful for their tireless efforts to bring about a safer, more humane world. Keep up the good and brave work! **Do not fail the children of Earth or their children! Dodi and I send our eternal flame of love to all in the spirit of peace-**

Diana, the Peacemaker and Ambassador of Peace!

Send the Peacekeepers! June 8, 2002

M: Di, it's me. I'm here to listen to your voice, and be your voice.

D: That's great Darling, I'm here to comment on world affairs, and there is much that needs our mutual attentions today.

M: Is there anything that needs our particular attention today?

D: It's hard to know where to begin! So much trouble everywhere, and so many possible outcomes.

We commend the efforts of the President and Mr. Mubarak, in their meetings. We regard the situation in the Middle East as the number one priority for the future of the entire world is at stake here. If a time line can be set up for the creation of the state of Palestine, Mr. Mubarak is so right in calling for this! Do this sooner than later, for the sake of your children, and your children's children. **It will do much to ease terror and tensions throughout the entire world. While at the same time, assist the people of both Palestine and Israel. We further recommend the Peace keeping forces to be sent in from the UN. That this would prove most helpful in deterring terror from the Palestinians and Israeli's. Israel need not agree with all the details now, but pressure needs to be put on her to give up some land for peace, and in turn the rewards to her security would be so much greater than anything she could possibly do right now in the way of peacekeeping!**

Arab nations and the US will have to do most of the negotiating, for Mr. Sharon and Mr. Arafat are not really going to do this for themselves. They must be led by the hand a bit, so to speak.

M: Di, that's brilliant. I really hope our diplomats can broker a peace deal with the help of the Arab nations. In this way, we'll be seen as a savior in the eyes of the Arab world, at least by some of the Arab states, and this will likely reduce the likelihood of the US being a target of terror again. Is there anything else for today, Di?

D: It is indeed a busy agenda, Darling. We'll move on in a moment. We want to express our gratitude again for your work on your new book, and the pictures you were able to come up with from my funeral. That Dodi and I are so pleased with your effort, and the beautiful book it is going to make!

M: It's a jewel in your crown of books, Diana. I am very pleased, too, to have collaborated on your words and wisdom. Is there anything else you wish to comment on at this point?

D: Yes, I'm getting there, Dearest. We see that in India and Pakistan that more needs to be done. Whilst continuing efforts of the diplomats are good, they aren't leading where they should, and the possibility of one of the skirmishes on the boarder breaking out into all-out war is very likely indeed. So we recommend that the highest level diplomats continue to work, behind the scenes if necessary, to stop the potential for war, and that some kind of agreement be drawn up between India and Pakistan, on the issue of Kashmir. That this scenario is another of the Al Qaeda's projects and they are behind some of the tensions between the two states. They are a menace to the whole human race!

M: Diana, you are saying a similar message to last week but I'm so glad to hear your advice. Is there anything else for today?

D: I'm closing shortly, Darling. We want the world to know that the war on terror will be won in time, through both the efforts of the Allied Nations in Afghanistan, and the diplomatic efforts in the Middle East. That all the diplomats involved in so many levels of negotiations are to be commended for their continued efforts. And we thank you as well for your efforts. **We want to save a world for you, and your children, and your children's children. This message is from Diana, the peacemaker and Princess of Peace. All my love in a troubled time,**

Diana

The Creation of Palestine is Crucial to World Peace! June 14, 2002

M: Di, it's me, I'm here to listen to your voice.

D: That's great Darling, we'll get started right away.

M: Is there anything you wish to address today? I know there is a lot of news out there.

D: Of course Darling, there is always an agenda, and a rather urgent one at that. Whilst there are many issues confronting the many diplomatic fronts occurring simultaneously throughout the world, we wish to commend the efforts of those diplomats involved in the India-Pakistan conflict in particular for their hard work. We are hoping that their efforts will have averted a possible nuclear war there, and for this they are highly commended. We also wish to say that the organization behind the bombing in [Karachi] Pakistan today is part of the entire radical extremist organization of the region to which I have referred to before. They are part of the Al Qaeda network and ascribe to the same Muslim extremist philosophy; hatred of the West and of anyone not like them. **That this immature thinking and behavior in the name of God is a total blaspheme upon the true Creator God, known to all Muslims as Allah. We in spirit wish to emphasize again that Allah, the Creator God, wills no violence upon innocent civilians at this time or any time.**

M: Agreed, Diana, and it is important to continue to stress this especially that you are in spirit, where the obvious truth about such things concerning our belief in God and understanding of his will is obvious. I want to comment on something I read yesterday. I read an article that involved Colin Powell's interest in Palestine and in creating the state of Palestine, if only temporary. I was so relieved to see that, Diana. He's on the right track, don't you think?

D: My heartfelt praise of Colin Powell's fine peace work is appropriate here. Mr. Powell knows from many sources that the creation of the state of Palestine is crucial to forming world peace at this time. If you nations will concentrate your effort on just this, so much bloodshed and terror will be averted. And this is just what I'm trying to do for Earth and her inhabitants right now, so as to assist the human race in reaching her goal of peace! And we need so many peace workers right now, for so many are led astray. The more light workers and peace workers we have working on a just solution for Palestine, the better. And those who work for peace in any way are greatly appreciated and regarded, even here in the spirit realm.

M: Di, I know there must be more. There is just so much news, and so many fires burning everywhere, literally and figuratively.

D: I'm closing shortly, and although there are many issues and fires burning, especially in Colorado, we in spirit see an end to that and hope that the wildfires don't spread out of control. Let us be clear that the need for peace workers is increasing due to the dark negative consciousness that is eroding Islam. If there needs to be more effort on the part of the Arab governments in reeducation for their respective states, so be it. So much of this is coming directly from the Mosques, and the Mullahs. Mr. Musharraf is quite correct in calling for reeducation in the regions of Pakistan. While on that note of Pakistan, we ask all reading these messages to continue to pray for peace amongst brethren in Pakistan and India, for the situation is still quite volatile. While some progress has been made, we still see a possibility for that progress to erode. Therefore, peace workers, be diligent in your continued efforts to quell violence especially at the borders! The peace workers of this world have nothing to fear in being of service to human kind, for in making peace you will not only save yourselves but your children, and your children's children. Be watchful in the times ahead, and vigilant. All my love to the world's peace-workers. Know my love is with you and I watch over you with special care,

Diana,

Princess of Peace

UN: Bring in the Peacekeepers for Israel/Palestine! June 18, 2002

M: Di, it's me. I'm here to listen to your voice, and be your voice if there is anything you wish to say.

D: That's great Darling. We'll get started now. Today I wish to address the increasing tensions in Israel/Palestine. That the recent suicide bombing in Jerusalem was so tragic at this crucial time, really. Our heartfelt sympathies extend to all the families who lost loved ones. We further wish to add that the creation of the Palestinian state still very much needs to be on the agenda for the US. For only in this way will the US deter further terror on the homeland front, by working for peace and justice for the Palestinian people.

M: I'm really worried that Israel will go in with further incursions, since so many lost lives (20 plus) and they are feeling threatened, with the need to suppress this sort of violence.

D: That is very likely indeed, and again will bring nothing but bloodshed and loss of human life, both Israeli and Palestinian. That their efforts are better served at the negotiating table than at the battlefield.

M: Agreed, Diana. I just wish there were an easier way, and I know from your words, there is!

D: Indeed there is! I am a light worker for the cause of Earth right now, and the Earth needs this work. You are very blessed to do this on my behalf. **Now then, what I so wish to**

emphasize is that the Peacekeepers from the UN need to be brought into the deal for the temporary, provisional state of Palestine. That the latest suicide bombing only further illustrates that the cry for help is indeed desperate for measures, which will keep this process of peace in check. I further wish to add that I have warned that as the process of peace nears its goals and agendas, there will be those extremist groups who do not want peace, and even appear to not want a Palestine! Beware in these troubled times ahead then, and do not let their terrible deeds frighten you out of peacemaking. For the goal of peace in that region is well worth the trouble and effort and will bring nothing but security and peace to both Israel and the United States, as well as her allies. That only in this way will the US secure her future, and the future of the whole human race!

M: Wow, you've said a great deal of wisdom, Diana. I want to bring something else to your attention here. There has been rumor and speculation that Colin Powell may resign midterm. And this would be so devastating to the peace process. They say he's getting all kinds of flack from other members of the cabinet who are less inclined to peace, or disagree with his fine peace agenda. Don't they see the advantages to Mr. Powell's peace agenda?

D: Mr. Colin Powell is doing a remarkable job of diplomacy, even in spite of his cabinet's disagreement with him. My advice to him is to stay the course and not give up, even in the face of apparent ridicule, and dissension. That he is right and that his interest in peace is in serving humanity's highest good. He is a man of integrity and vision, and he must hold to the vision of the Palestinian state, and not waver. For he is at his appointed hour, and his finest moment! For this will further his popularity and his position personally as well as globally! He and the world can only gain; so press on the good fight!

M: The President, Mr. Bush, is supposed to announce the creating of a provisional Palestine sometime this week. Everyone is worried that he'll back down, give in to the latest terrorist bombings, and assume that Arafat can't lead because he can't control terror factions.

D: That is all quite correct. It is Mr. Powell's prerogative to persuade Mr. Bush not to give in to terror, just as in his (Mr. Bush's) rhetoric which he repeats to his own people, the United States, not to give in to terror! That more terror can't thwart the peace process! I have repeatedly warned of them (the terrorist extremists) doing this, just to disrupt the peace process!

Really, the terrorists can't win! And clearly Israel can't win either with this constant state of terror and turmoil. She will fare much better with the boarders drawn up and the rights of the Palestinian people restored to them. I am closing shortly. We in spirit salute and bow to the noble peace workers doing this difficult work. We ask continued strength in the face of apparent disappointment, and to stay the course for peace! All my love to all the Peace workers doing this noble work,

Diana,

Princess of Peace!

Bring the Peacekeepers to the Region! June 22, 2002

M: Hi, Di, it's me. I'm here to listen to your voice and be your voice if there is anything you wish to say.

D: That's great Darling. We're glad to hear from you. We so wish to emphasize what a lovely art show you had yesterday, and we were pleased with the many people you reached with your art, and the many comments that were made about me as well. We feel your art will be a true success as time goes by and the book is published, which won't be too much longer, by the way!

M: Di, that is great. I'm encouraged by your words, which are so very lovely as usual!

D: Rightly should it be so, since you deserve compliments for your excellence. Now then, I wish to return to world affairs, as there is much that needs our mutual attention today.

M: Indeed, there is increasing tension in the West Bank and Gaza, and the situation appears serious Di, is there anything you wish to recommend?

D: I know I must sound repetitive, but the presence of the Peacekeeping forces needs to be brought in to prevent the presence of the suicide bombers, and to also oversee the fairness of the Israeli's as they search for terrorists in the Palestinian territories. That the creating of a Palestinian state will need the Peacekeepers to enforce the peace while negotiations are going on; and if this measure is taken with the help of Mr. Annan, then the creation of Palestine will go forward more smoothly. I have repeatedly warned of the dire consequences of the peace process: that many factions just don't want peace, and to work through the bombings none-the less. But we in spirit see that the presence of the UN peacekeepers would do much to deter terror in the region.

M: Thank you, Diana. I know that some who get this message may consider your words, and perhaps pursue that as an option, and a very excellent one. Do you wish me to try to contact the UN, perhaps anonymously?

D: That would be excellent Darling, and would make a difference, even if those delivering the message don't believe it, nonetheless, the ideas need to be seen in words. That this will help deter terror in the entire region, and so why not use the idea?

M: On another point, Diana, there seems to be another terror threat from Osama Bin Laden, and we are worried here in the States. Do you consider this a viable threat, and what should we do to prepare for this? If you know anything please let us know.

D: The weapons of mass destruction is their evil plan, and most of these as your Administration well knows, are stored in Iraq. **But the Al Qaeda network has threatened many things, and from our point of view, as I have said to Americans, so many times in these messages, to take cover!** Be especially careful on the fourth of July, your independence holiday, and be careful on the airplanes in the weeks ahead. We see that they may be planning another hijacking, perhaps from Europe, to enter the United States, and then strike with the weapons (of mass destruction) in some way. Their obvious targets are major cities, like Washington, DC and other major cities. They have so many plots that they change them every day. This, in general, is what I have warned about in the past; some form of chemical, biological or nuclear terror from the airplanes! It is well to consider their threats as credible, and that the person Osama Bin Laden is still planning evil against the US.

M: Diana, it is well to consider your warnings as credible as well. When you warned us in the fall of 2001, you said, "All Americans' Take Cover" and of course, there was the shoe bomber three months later. So we appreciate your help even though it is very difficult to be more specific.

Is there anything else you wish to comment on?

D: I think this message is a good summary for now. I do wish to say that the incursions by Israeli tanks again into the Palestinian territories is not good for peace. And they must be stopped so that the Summer Peace Summit can continue. The Peacekeepers need to be brought in to speed up the stalled process. That we salute and bow to all those who work for peace wherever they are! For they are the true royalty at this time, and we ask your continued prayers for peace. That this message is from Diana, Princess of Peace for your world in a troubled time!

All my love, Diana.

Commendation to Mr. Bush and Mr. Powell for Palestine! June 28, 2002

M: Hi Di, it's me. I'm late but here to listen to your voice.

D: That's great Darling. We've been watching you create your latest masterpiece. We so wish to say that it's one of the nicest paintings of me you've created so far, and we're very pleased. It will do much to afford the world a look at my personality whilst they can view your talent as well. (See XI. Diana Mother Comfort, page 43, or go to the web site to view it in color, at **www.dianaspeakstotheworld.com/diana_speaks/**)

M: Well, I'm glad to hear you think I'm improving my painting. I love it and you, and this one says much for your compassion and kindness, Diana.

D: You're really too sweet, but thank you.

M: Well, Diana, another week has come and gone, and there is so much going on. First of all, they're going to create Palestine, and I'm happy to hear that, aren't you?

D: We're thrilled that they finally got the idea out of the box, so to speak. We find things in the President's plan that may or may not be feasible, but we're so relieved they didn't squelch the plan entirely, you see the other members of the cabinet had such a hard time, really, with this idea.

However, the President and Mr. Powell feel certain that this will do much to ease the suffering there, and at the same time, bring the Arab nations into a wider circle of friendship with the United States, thereby leaving the possibility of dealing with terror in the region.

M: You mean, dealing with Iraq and the threat of nuclear, biological or chemical terror?

D: Precisely, Darling. They feel that Palestine will help the friendship enlarge so that even while the moderate Arab nations won't necessarily be in support of any kind of attack on Iraq, they will perhaps be in support in other ways. They rightly want all the support they can get in the war on terror and particularly in the area of weapons of mass destruction.

M: I see. And it all makes sense, Diana. I am wondering why they are setting the deadline for Palestine to three years or more. It seems so crucial now to get her off the ground and running, especially from what you have said in the past about the essential quality of creating Palestine. Any recommendations here, Diana?

D: Yes, we in spirit recommend that they reconsider such an arbitrary and late date. If they wait that long there may not be a world as we know it. It is possible that the weapons of mass destruction will be used in the meantime, so that all the possible agendas they want to project will not be brought forth. As I have said before in so many ways, Palestine needs your urgent attention.

That with a Palestinian state, the likelihood of further terror on US soil is negligible, compared to without

a Palestine, the likelihood is, well, 100%. To put it bluntly, they have no choice but to create Palestine, and Israel will need pressure on her to do this deal. To get the Arab states to back this plan, revisions will be necessary, I'm sure they realize. We want to emphasize that all efforts so far are indeed commendable, and that the US is on the right track, so to speak. But Palestine cannot wait. The **Muslim world is building up rhetoric and anger towards the West and only in this way will that be tempered by them seeing the United States wholeheartedly engaged in the welfare of a poor and Muslim nation such as Palestine, will they be able to view the absurdity of their rhetoric, and change their minds**. They have very few capable speakers who are free to speak about the rampant fundamentalism, which is so ruining the beautiful faith known as Islam. Dodi again wishes to say to be warned, not to buy into the prevalent thinking, which is terror and rhetoric against the West. That the west and east and in between, Middle East, will do better to tolerate the views of those not like you, than to promulgate doctrines which are a falsehood and fall directly out of line with Islam.

Mr. Musharraf has indeed done a commendable service to his countrymen in condemning the rampant spread of Muslim fanaticism, but there is still much of this widespread throughout the world. And this is as much the enemy as are those terrorists, who are backed by this rhetoric.

M: Wow, Diana, you've given a scholarly analysis of the situation, and far better than the author I saw on ***Lou Dobbs Moneyline*** (CNN) last night, who had absolutely no clue to what Muslim fundamentalism was all about. Thank you, and thank you to Dodi. Is there anything else, Diana?

D: I'm closing shortly. We feel that you are accelerating quickly with a creative fervor, and we are pleased that you are in tune with the whole of earth which is vibrating more quickly. You will find your dreams manifesting more quickly for you, and that your scope of influence, through me, will widen your horizons. We are also impressed with the whole of humanity, and whilst there is much to learn at such a difficult time, we want the human race to quicken her pace towards ascension, towards wholeness, towards peace. So that there is no suffering anywhere, and the nations will live in harmony and peaceful co-habitation. **We so wish a Palestine, and sooner rather than later, so that this vision can be a reality for the people of the world. One world, one God, one People, under Heaven, United in Common understanding and Peace. This will one day be the pledge to the people of Earth, for Earth and of the people.**

That this message is from Diana, the People's Princess, and Lightworker for Earth!

10. Diana, May You Stay Forever Young, watercolor, © 2002 Marcia McMahon. This is my commemorative birthday painting for Diana, completed on July 3, 2002, her 37th in 1997.

Diana's Words on Her Painting Just Completed July 3, 2002

(This was spontaneously channeled by Diana after completing a painting of her from her last birthday, July 1,1997. I completed the art today, July 3, 2002)

D: I am truly so deeply honored to have you bring forth my memory with such beauty, an artist's touch so sensitive, Darling!

M: Thanks Di, I'm really happy with your birthday painting. It seem to effervesce with joy, freshness, aliveness!

D: Indeed, it does Darling! We're so very pleased and indeed very grateful to have you! In so many ways, you bring forth my essence!

M: I'm so happy about the dream I had. You were meeting me for the day in a new outfit, which I liked.

D: You are afforded a glimpse of my afterlife endeavor. I am a busy woman here; and you so wish we could be friends on a day to day basis. Just know that you are a friend to me now, just as I too wish I had known you while I was alive. I'm honored to know you now Darling and that's really all that matters! Be at peace in your day.

M: About the terror that is being planned, can you offer any suggestions?

D: You've really done all you could. Colin (Powell) is aware of the situation, he's on it! The whole US intelligence is on it. Nothing may happen on the 4th. It's all entirely a matter of chance I am afraid to say.

M: Thank you, Diana. Let's hope nothing happens.

Palestine is the Key to Winning the War on Terror July 5, 2002

M: Di, it's me. I'm here to listen to your voice, and be your voice if there is anything you wish to say.

D: Great to hear from you, Darling. We have much that needs our mutual attentions. And we are pleased with your beautiful paintings that you've completed and framed. They are lovely tributes to my memory as Diana, Princess of Wales.

M: Diana, after watching, *Diana, Legacy of a Princess,* I see that the continuity of your humanitarian endeavor lives on through this work now. I see a progression of you from Land Mines and the Halo trust, to world peace, in the Middle East.

D: Most definitely, and it's for the people of Earth that I'm doing this work now.

M: No rest for the saintly!

D: Thank you for your compliment, we'll move on to world affairs, which need our mutual attentions. There is so much happening now; it seems to move from one crisis to the next.

We in spirit wish to emphasize that we feel that the act committed yesterday at the LAX airport terminal was terror related. We feel that may be uncovered in the ongoing investigation.

M: It certainly appears that way and has all the elements of a terrorist act. We in the States are hesitant to call it that, as if the obvious weren't obvious enough, I guess!

D: Well put Darling. We'll move along now to other serious issues.

M: What do you think about the progress in Palestine/Israel and about the possible attack on Iraq that was just released?

D: Precisely my agenda Darling, you're getting better at reading my mind. The process at hand is a bit backwards, as the US strongly needs the Arab allies in the region to win any kind of war in Iraq, and basically without Palestine, it won't work as well. We see a more efficient use of time in waging Peace instead of more war; especially our concern here and now is the Iraqi people, who deserve no more punishment. They have had enough punishment from the regime of Saddam Hussein, and feel so helpless to help themselves. They crave new leadership and new freedoms. We wish to recommend that a different route or strategy, that of sweeping political reforms be enacted instead of war, although we recognize that the US is on to them about the weapons of mass destruction I have repeatedly warned about!

M: Di, it's something you have warned about since November or December of last year. And if you can imagine, they haven't been inspected since 1998. No telling what they have in store.

D: Whilst the US is right in asking for a cessation of making of weapons of mass destruction, what **I am recommending is that they go in carefully and dismantle Sadam's infrastructure of mass destruction, cause a political coup if they like, and then let the people go. We see a possible outcome of World War if the US uses armed forces against Iraq! And we want to prevent that.**

M: Whoa, Diana, I am really worried about that. You said that with the invasion of Afghanistan, and still we see the mounting hatred of the West, the extremist rhetoric being touted as basic Muslim teachings in some states, and so I see your point. Is there anything else you wish to comment on at this time?

D: Yes, Dearest, there are other issues. We feel that the State of Palestine needs to be the number one top priority for the US and UN to focus on, as well as dealing with the delicate matter of Saddam Hussein. **We so wish to urge the diplomats who read my words to see to the creating of Palestine sooner rather than later, so as to truly win the war on "rhetoric" which is behind so much of the terror being perpetrated in the name of Allah.** And we ask that the Summer Summit, which was being talked about and touted as the solution to the problem, be allowed to continue. Ask the Prince of Saudi Arabia to lead it, let the US representatives go and urge the Arab states in on the deal. In that way, air bases and military strength can be given where it is needed. **Otherwise we see a very dismal scenario of possible nuclear war on Israel and the US, and very simply put, no one needs that!**

We so wish to emphasize the importance of Palestine, to end so much of the misery there for both Israelis and Palestinians, and sooner rather than later. This message is from Diana, Princess of Peace for your world. All my love in a troubled time,

Diana.

We in Spirit Are Looking Over America, and We Ask Caution with Iraq July 13, 2002

M: Di, it's me. I'm here to listen to your voice, and be your voice if there is anything you wish to say.

D: That's great Darling. We've been expecting to hear from you. There is much that needs our mutual attentions today.

M: I knew it. And of course, I've had many questions, especially concerning Palestine, the situation with England's ruling on remarriage of divorcees and Charles and Camilla. I wonder if you had anything to say on that matter, Diana?

D: Well, from my standpoint here, I only wish happiness for Charles at this time. My boys deserve the attentions of a true mother, and in this, I am a bit concerned about Camilla. But, it is entirely out of my control. We in spirit see that this is a very likely possibility for Charles now, and want him happy. I'm afraid I can't comment further now, Darling. We'll move on to world affairs.

M: Yes, is there a specific issue you wish to address Diana? And, I'm sorry if I brought up a personal issue, if I brought you any pain, for I would never do that.

D: That's fine Darling. There are many issues of concern for us in the realm of world affairs. I so wish to emphasize the importance of diplomacy in the weeks ahead with regard to Iraq, and with regard to Palestine. We so wish to emphasize again that the State of Palestine needs your urgent attentions. We recommend a Summer Summit, even if only for the purpose of further peace discussions, and to bring in the Arab states, to make them aware that they indeed have a voice and power in the region, beyond that of just the United States. We want to stress the importance of the Peacekeepers for Israel at this time, that this idea be proposed by someone in authority at the Summit. That the Summit can't wait another year, too many lives will be pointlessly given up to violence, and the increasing tensions in the region bear this out.

M: Diana, what about the buildup of tensions in the Arab world, and Iraq? Is it possible that some of the less moderate Arab states will side with Iraq or perpetrate more terror if we just go in and invade Iraq?

D: As I have repeatedly warned, we see drastic consequences to the outright invasion of Iraq due to the tensions in the area and the radical extremist groups that would erupt in further terror! We therefore caution the US and her allies against outright force and ask that they get intelligence operative in Iraq and Iran, and instead focus on toppling the regime of Sadam Hussein from within his own ranks. That allowing a coup to occur would be much more productive, then the weapons of mass destruction could be dealt with by destruction afterward and possibly in a more open way, though that would have to be determined. We see that the regime is very weakened by these reports and rumors of war, and that many of the people of both Iraq and Iran want freedom and democracy; and they are entitled to peace, not war upon their heads just because they are subject to dictatorial regimes. We see more productive results from diplomacy and intelligence operatives in those respective countries, and fewer casualties as well.

M: Diana, I heard that Arafat has written a long letter to Colin Powell, and we don't know the exact contents but they say it involves democracy and peace for Palestine. Perhaps he really is genuine at least in his desire for peace for his people, and in asking the intervention of Mr. Powell?

D: We in spirit have said all along that Mr. Arafat is genuine in his desire for peace and that he is not a terrorist. While some of his practices in the past have had that overtone, we feel that because he is an older man, with a child now, he is more in line with peace than anything else. That he is not condoning these horrible acts of terror, which are continuing in Israel. And that his people need to be given a chance to create the state of Palestine, that this would ease much of the tensions. But that at the moment, they do in fact need the Peacekeepers!

M: One more question. Some psychics have warned that Osama bin Laden wants to perpetrate nuclear war on America, and that if he gets to Iran or Iraq that will be his evil game plan. Do you see any possibility of this occurring or can you comment on this?

D: We in spirit see that that is his desire, and we wish no further comment on that evildoer. That it is the job of the intelligence agencies to find him and capture him before he can commit this outrageous scheme. And that we feel he will be caught in time. We so wish to emphasize that if the US will use her Ambassadors for peace—Mr. Colin Powell included—

for her best objectives, [by focusing] on Palestine and on intelligence in Iraq and Iran, things will turn out right. With a more militant approach, the other side will be militant as well, and that is the real fear. Therefore make no war on Iraq or Iran just yet, and try all other means before resorting to this mode of operation. **That we in spirit are indeed looking over the great country America, and Britain as well, for the good of all the people of Earth.** This message is from Diana, the peoples Princess, for the people of Earth at this time.

All my love in a troubled time, Diana.

Diplomacy Urged for Iraq July 20, 2002

M: Hi, Di, it's me. I'm here to listen to your voice and be your voice.

D: That's great, Darling. We've been waiting for your call. We've much that needs our mutual attentions today.

M: Concerning world affairs, no doubt?

D: Of course! We are so pleased at the recent conference on peace held at the United Nations with General Secretary Annan and Secretary Powell, and all the Arab delegates. We feel that much progress is being made for peace, and we highly commend the efforts of Mr. Powell, Mr. Annan and the Arab leaders as well. For all can work together for peace for our world.

It is indeed sad to see the continued suffering in Israel/Palestine, with another suicide bombing and the continuing of incursions. That this needs to end sooner [rather] than later, so that the suffering of the people there, both Israeli and Palestinian, may come to an end. We recognize the ardent efforts of so many working for peace, yourself included. For while you simply record my words, you've really no idea how helpful this really is to those diplomats who read my words.

And we feel you should ask for rewards for your work in some way, so as to be able to continue with this selfless service in lieu of returning to your former full time profession, which would only pull you further away your true calling, which is writing and art! So have faith that this avenue will shortly open for you, and you will be well rewarded!

M: Diana, thank you for mentioning that. It was really kind of you. Yes this is truly my one passion now, and I feel that my hard work does merit some reward. The publisher is so very slow in getting this important book out, and it might be another six months to a year, meanwhile those who might benefit from your messages are made to wait. I don't think the importance of your words can wait, Diana!

D: No, indeed. For I am privileged to share from my heavenly vantage point, which is far more encompassing than most working psychics even here on earth. I have explained before that we enjoy a kind of TV, whereby we view the possible outcomes to the political scenarios of nations.

My main interest in these continuing messages is to bring this important material to those who may benefit from it, in such a way as to wage peace for the nations involved, and to further my humanitarian causes from where I am now. For indeed our causes continue beyond so called death, if that is what we choose to do with our time here.

M: Diana, you are truly the same wonderful Princess we all love. And my gratitude to you for this selfless service is immeasurable.

D: Darling, you really are too kind. Now we'll move back to today's message. I wish to emphasize that Palestine is still the number one top priority, and the sooner she is created, the greater the sense of homeland security for Israel, the United States, and Palestine! We rejoice in this week's meeting with the diplomats and we so highly commend the efforts of the peace worker Colin Powell, as well as the efforts of Mr. Bush. Mr. Powell has done a commendable job of educating the members of his cabinet of the importance of Palestine, and is working on a fine solution to the security issues with regards to the Arab state's involvement. Bravo!

We so wish to emphasize that this one step, in creating Palestine will do much to deter terror in the region and in the US as well. It is our hope that the US can also further the cause for new leadership in Iraq without an outright invasion into that country, which we see would be disastrous in terms of loss of human life. We strongly urge the Allied forces to use restraint and not to go in there just yet, to exhaust all possible diplomatic efforts and covert efforts before doing this. This approach will strengthen the image of the United States amongst the Arab nations and win their support. And will increase the security in the Middle East, thereby increasing trust and mitigating the effects of rampant terror, which so afflict that region. We salute and bow to all the royalty doing this fine peace work, on behalf of earth right now. This message is from Diana, Princess of peace for your world.

All my love to the peace workers! Diana

A Request for UN Peacekeepers in Israel/Palestine July 26, 2002

M: Di, it's me, here to listen to your voice and be your voice if there is anything you wish to say.

D: That's great Darling. We were hoping you would be feeling well enough to do this work. If not, you may rest one more day and then begin. Are you really feeling up to this?

M: I'm very tired, but I am ok. Thank you, Diana.
Do go on.

D: Very well then, Darling. We'll send on healing energies as you write.

M: Thank you Diana. I know there have been issues you've been patiently waiting to speak on all week.

D: Thank you, for your interest and kindness. We regret the further loss of life in Palestine, especially the killing of innocent civilians in the recent Israeli F-16 attack that killed a major terrorist from Hamas, and also so many children! We in spirit are grieved those children are being dragged into this, and that Israel felt they had to do this. **That this outright aggression must be stopped, and the United Nations and other humanitarian groups should call for an end to this madness!**

M: Right, Diana, for it makes them no better than the suicide bombers in a way, since they are taking out innocent civilians. I understand from the news that they felt they had to take this person out, since he was a major terrorist, behind many of the suicide bombings.

D: Indeed that is true, and yet it is so unfortunate for the innocent children! We in spirit see that if Israel isn't stopped from this kind of invasion into the Gaza strip and the West Bank this will become a modus operandi, a means of controlling terror on the home front which is a clear violation of the rights of the Palestinian people (who aren't involved in terror.) I am speaking for the Palestinians at this juncture, for their lot has been so tortured and difficult already. Their suffering has been so great and that of the Israelis as well. We ask the diplomats involved to set up some form of humanitarian watch dog group, so as to monitor this kind of behavior on the part of recognized governments. And it certainly isn't going to help the already fomenting terror in the region.

M: I saw where the Islamic groups have vowed revenge. And this kind of thing incites them to more revenge. The whole process seems to lead from violence to more violence. The only solution has to be political: creating Palestine, with a peacekeeping force of some kind in place to watch over both nations as Palestine emerges.

D: Darling, very well put. And we see that the presence of the Peacekeepers would strengthen the whole region, and also function as a watchdog group, to best protect the Palestinian people, who really have no real protection at all. We also commend the words of the US President in condemning this kind of outright attack on Palestine. He is so right in this! We just wish that there would be more action behind his words, in the sense of installing the Peacekeepers.

M: You mean getting the UN more involved than it presently is, which right now, has been the peace talks that were recently held in New York. They can't do everything at once. Things have to be talked out first. And really they are just forming the right conditions so as to get the process going, Diana. You know this, but for the sake of clarity here I am mentioning this.

D: Yes, we are well aware of the fine peacemaking efforts of the diplomats, and in particular the efforts of Mr. Powell, who is doing so much for Palestine right now. We commend his action highly, and ask that all efforts be exhausted so as to prevent further terror like what happened this week, so it does not become a pattern and the norm (on the part of Israel), for we see that would not benefit the peace process at all. And Israel strongly defends her right to self-defense, which your President understands, but at the same time there is no one who can defend the helpless Palestinian people. Who really are the victims in all of this, and who aren't involved in terror. I am of course speaking in terms of the average Palestinian who right now, can't hold a job, and can't feed their families due to the region of terror that the Israeli military is clamping down on the people there!

M: I can't imagine the horror of just living there, in either Palestinian refugee camps or in Israel for that matter. I know Israel has all the benefits of a modern nation, and Palestine has nothing.

D: That is basically it, their basic needs are hardly being met and it is a humanitarian crisis that is growing in proportion to the vast escalation of military operations in the West bank and Gaza. We see this as counter-productive and want to preserve the opportunity for peace in the region. We ask that the diplomats recommend the watch dog groups be allowed to come in and observe, perhaps the United Nations. Although we know they were denied entry into Jenin.

M: If it will help deter this kind of thing and help the living conditions of the average Palestinian, those not involved in terror in their daily lives, yes, it seems a good idea, Diana.

D: I am closing shortly. We pray for peace for Palestine and Israel. We commend the efforts of Peace Workers everywhere, and we ask for the involvement of the diplomats to deter the actions of Israel's military so we don't see more of this in the future. We ask that more humanitarian aid be allowed into Palestine, to help the many suffering there. We commend the peace workers everywhere. This message is from the peace worker Diana, Princess of peace for Earth at this time.

All my love, Diana

Stop All Violence in the Name of Religious Vengeance! August 2, 2002

D: My message of peace is unfolding shortly. Thank you for your steadfast commitment to peace.

M: I'm here for you Di, if there is anything you wish to say for today, to listen to you and be your voice as well.

D: That's great, Darling. There is much in the Middle East situation that needs our mutual attentions. That we in spirit so regret the loss of American lives in Israel, especially those of students, who really bring home the issue of cooperation and oneness so well in a thriving university situation (Hebrew University) like that. When we see these lives shattered so easily for nothing, for no good cause, it causes me to grieve as well. Even though we know that all life is eternal and goes on forever, the students who were killed are having a difficult time in accepting their deaths due to this unprecedented violence. It says in your Holy Scripture, "An eye for an eye, a tooth for a tooth," and so on, and you know this kind of vengeance is what is being played out. Ancient Hebrew scribes, Middle Eastern peoples who formed for us all the basic texts of your early Bible, wrote those words. And we regret to say that mankind hasn't yet evolved out of the most basic level of understanding! Even in the words of your great teacher Jesus, who proclaimed love over evil and vengeance, this hasn't yet impressed upon you the need to stop all violence in the name of God and religious wars. This religious vengeance must stop, and all hatreds and all vengeance must surely come to an end. By means of reeducation in the entire region, and in particular the Mid East region so that Jews do not grow up hating Muslims, and Muslims hating Jews. Because this rhetoric about hating the West, and hating the Jews and Christians must stop! **Dodi again wishes to say to his people, not to buy into the rhetoric so prevalent in the region, the hatred of Jews and Christians, which this is clearly out of line with true Islam. And he asks all violence in the name of Allah to stop!**

M: Diana, I am pausing for a moment. What you have said, and Dodi has said is beautiful, and so eloquently right. That is the most I've heard you say in one breath in a long time. Have you any recommendations politically?

D: Of course, Darling, and we'll get to that. The sooner the Peacekeepers can be brought in to restore order, the better. That we feel they will be able to stop this madness that Israel has begun by sending in tanks and troops. That this escalation will only stall the longed for peace process, and the diplomats need to take immediate action to persuade Israel to forgo the extravagant use of force on the peoples of the West Bank and Gaza. Surely, she must realize that will cause more and more terror and rebellion from the extremists such as Hamas, who clearly don't want peace. That this escalation on the part of Israel will cause an all-out war zone there among the Palestinians and Jews, with continued bloodshed and loss of life, interruption to the economy and great expense to Israel, with no real consequences. For the terror won't stop. Not with continued occupation and harassment of many innocent men who are not involved in terror. What we in spirit see is just the continuation of this bloodbath, until a political state can be put in place, namely Palestine. **As we have said before,**

Palestine will do much to deter terror in the region and worldwide terror on Americans. We so wish the peace process to continue and we so hate the barbaric crimes of those responsible for the latest bombing in Jerusalem at Hebrew University. **For our youth are our hopes for the future, and when we destroy them, we destroy our own hopes and dreams!**

We ask that immediate steps be taken to expedite all matters that pertain to the creating of a Palestine, and that the incursions in Israel be brought to a stop. We further wish to recommend that the Peacekeepers be brought in as soon as it becomes feasible to do so, that this will help so much in the interim phases of Palestine. And we commend those who work for peace, so tirelessly, yourself included. And we bow and salute to the royalty doing this noble peace work for the world at this time and we ask them not to tire nor give in to political pressures or demands from either side in the matter, to stride forward with this noble cause and not give in to terror. **This message is from Diana, Princess of Peace for Earth at this time.**

All my love in a troubled time, Diana

An Extraordinary Message from Michael and Diana by Robert Murray

This just came over the inter net to me in my mailbox. It seems to make all my efforts worthwhile for peace with Diana at my side. Dear reader, I hope you are able to bear with me, for it is both a message of great joy and affirmation, and something, which I debated about sharing with you. I affirm the heart connection with Diana as a true friend, and this verifies the unique connection that we now share. I'm already in my next book, Princess Diana's Message of Peace, book II, and I hope to share more with you, including messages from Mother Teresa!

Hi Marcia,

I do believe you will find this QUITE interesting. This is from a message my father received today from Michael. Got your Diana message - thanks! I also just got your other message and will read that. Anyway, hope you're ready for what is below.

Bye for now & take care, James Murray

Illustrator, *The Stars Still Shine: An Afterlife Journey*

Message from Michael

November 16, 2002 4:25 P.M.

"Hello! Lots of developments since I talked to you last. Diana is into the peace thing in a big way. As she explained it, if there isn't peace then all the children are at risk in all countries. She keeps talking about Earth Angel Marcia. She told me that it was okay to tell Marcia what I tell you.

However, when she was over at Essex a few days ago, she was telling me all about George W. Bush, Mr. Powell and Tony Blair. I was interested, but sometimes her intensity on the subject of peace drives some of us to distraction. It's not that we don't want peace or help for the children; it's just that we have our own ways of dealing with problems. Diana understands what we are feeling and what we are saying, but she is driven to do something about it right now. Marcia is her right arm right now, Diana said. Diana has now left the building.

Love to all, Mike.
xxx ooo Lynn and Emily."[10]

[10] This excerpt used with permission from Robert Murray, author, The Stars Still Shine: An Afterlife Journey.
© 2000. Aura Publishing, Derby Line, Vermont
www.TheStarsStillShine.com)

Epilogue
Diana is Still "Queen of Hearts"

Diana tells me this is not really the end of the book. That with every end, there is a new beginning. So I look forward to another channeled book with Diana as my guide. Everything about this adventure in channeling Diana has been fascinating for me. From her first words to me in May of 2001, when she said she'd like me to be an "Ambassador for Peace" in my part of the world, to her numerous calls for Peace Accords in the Middle East. First of all, let it be said here that Diana is the real Ambassador for Peace, and this is how she signs her letters. I'm just a good listener to the Princess of Peace and very glad to be involved in her endeavor on behalf of peace for the world at this momentin time!

Two testimonials I regard as my jewels in the crown of my "Diana" messages are from author Robert Murray, who occasionally receives messages from Diana, too. His book, ***"The Stars Still Shine: An Afterlife Journey,"*** is the journey of his deceased son in law Michael. Michael has a quote from Diana in which she acknowledges my hard work (see "A Confirmation of Diana"), and then the message at the very end of this book, titled, "***An Extraordinary Message from Michael and Diana.***" Well, it has been a pleasure to work with and for Diana, and to befriend both James and Bob Murray. Diana is the hard worker and gets the credit for this book, a labor of love for both of us, yes, if you can save a world from self-extinction. Diana says, "Make peace now, for your children, and your children's children," from her channeled messages dated February, 2002.

Thanks

I wish to thank Dorothy May Mercer for her selfless service to helping with the publication of this 2nd edition of Princess Diana's Message of Peace.

Dorothy Mercer is a true angel and a gifted author, editor and helpful consultant. Without Dorothy I would never have been able to complete this 2nd edition of Princess Diana's Message of Peace. She has labored tireless hours and is very gifted as a writer's consultant. Please find her and her wonderful books, mysteries and adventure series on the web at

Mercer, Dorothy. www.Mercerpublications.com books bargains and more!

I'd like to thank my heart friend Maria, whose tireless hours of web site design were absolutely essential to the success of the messages of Diana and my web site, Diana Speaks to the World.

www.dianaspeakstotheworld.com

You can also see my Diana Gallery I and II and purchase a print of one of my paintings from the book. They are full original size 11x17" and really beautiful!

My web site is a real beauty thanks to Maria's ability with graphics, web design and the use of my paintings as well. If you ever get a chance, go to her web site at Princess Diana: A Journey into My Heart at:

www.angelfire.com/mb/mariadianapage

Her marvelous poetry and graphics depict the Diana we all loved and treasured, in all her varieties of mood and beauty. Her site has won numerous awards for its magnificence.

For some it's difficult to accept that Diana is working through me, someone they formerly knew as an artist and art teacher. For others, it's difficult that Diana chose an American over say, someone from Wales. I have some thoughts on that which I'll share now. First of all, with all channeling, the lovely spirit of Diana came to me, and this is how it works.

There have been other Diana channels, one of my favorites being of course, Rita Eide. Rita is in Norway, and her book is channeled in English. Rita's book, her first from Diana, titled ***The Celestial Voice of Diana: Her Spiritual Guidance to Finding Love***, published by Findhorn Press in Scotland, was not widely welcomed for publication in England. The Royal Family has consulted psychics for a long time, but does not formally acknowledge channeling. While I've done all I can to respect the privacy of the Royal Family, there are incidental references to them. Diana is still a mother to both William and Harry, and sends on her eternal love and protection to her two sons in these messages.

Why isn't there a channel from Wales? I have my ideas; perhaps you have your own. I make no apologies for the fact that there aren't any, at least to my knowledge at this writing.

Why America, and why me, of all Americans? I believe that Diana came to me in spirit because I'm an American, and that this message was designed to reach other Americans who can have an impact on the War on Terror. I'm helping my country, the United States, and the world with this message and that is just what Diana wanted. With her numerous references to Mr. Powell, Mr. Blair and Mr. Bush it's quite clear to me who Diana is speaking to in these messages. She wants this material to reach the top people, many of the same people she knew in her life as Diana, Princess of Wales. Diana was a good friend of Colin Powell in life, and is in fact distantly related to Mr. Powell. Is it just possible that she is looking after the wellbeing of an entire nation, and entire world, through her words to Mr. Powell and others? I believe she is. You'll have to make up your own mind. That is what I always recommend with channeling, read with an open mind and heart, and then decide what rings true for you!

As a dear friend says, my artwork speaks volumes about my love for the person of Diana. I have worked so very hard on this book and my artwork of Diana. Diana chose me, I think because she must trust me, she knew of my art ability, and when spirits cross over they can view the lifetimes of other people. Diana already knew of my other books, yet to be published, and of my art ability, so she's obviously looked into my life in the records, the so-called Akashic records. So she apparently wanted my artwork to grace this book, and I'm totally delighted to bring forth her beauty once more!

I have to thank Rita Eide because without Rita's book, *The Celestial Voice of Diana,* I might not ever have known Diana. My continuing gratitude goes to author Robert Murray, whose delightful book about Michael's afterlife, *The Stars Still Shine: An Afterlife Journey*, has contributed so much additional information to my understanding and work with Diana. This book contains important information about the afterlife, and features Diana's words as written through Michael. I also wish to thank Alice Bateman, editor and owner of ***The Writer's Voice***, the world's largest literary forum, for publishing my many Diana messages and for her support!

Diana's absolutely like a close and trusted friend. This is what she said to Harry, in her letter, June 2001 that I am "like a good friend to Mummy now!" I was so touched really! So I don't think that this friendship will ever really end. I have been privileged to be part of a miracle, of knowing Princess Diana in her afterlife endeavor, and to help bring her voice of peace to the war torn world. I am a peace worker for Diana.

Who could ask for a more satisfying assignment, or a more challenging one?

Diana, I want to say how much I love you, and all of what you stood for in your short but lovely life on Earth as Princess Diana. And Diana, how much brilliance you have at peace work! May we all use your wisdom and apply it to the world situation, before it's too late.

I know that we'll meet again, and be good friends over there, but meanwhile, remember I'm still here to be your voice. "Don't worry Darling, this isn't your last assignment," she is saying now. For as she said her famous speech when she tried to withdraw from public life, in 1993, **"Wherever there is suffering, wherever there is pain, just call on me and I'll be there in an instant. I want to be there as a Queen of Hearts!"**

Diana, Princess of Wales.

Author's Biography

Marcia McMahon BA, Ursuline College
MA, Case Western Reserve University
And The Cleveland Institute of Art

Marcia McMahon is an artist and author and has her art in private collections throughout the US and Europe. She was recently named in Who's Who in America for 2002 and 2003 for her accomplish-ments in art teaching and art exhibition, which she has done for more than 20 years. Her messages from Princess Diana were featured on a *September 11th Anthology Channeling web site* at **(www.spiritlite.com)** and Marcia is featured among leading names in spirituality, among them Neale Donald Walsch, Annie Kirkwood and Robert Murray.

Marcia gives readings of Princess Diana's Messages which are quite powerful, as well as radio and TV interviews. To request her in your area, email Marcia

Marciadi2002@yahoo.com

Go to her web site at:

www.dianaspeakstotheworld.com

To order artwork of Princess Diana, go to the Diana Gallery I,II thruXI.www.dianaspeakstotheworld.com/mb2/diana_speaks/gallery_index.html

Princess Diana's Charities

- British Red Cross,
  9 Grovsvenor Crescent , London SVOIX7EJ

- Centerpoint, (temporary assistance to the homeless) Freepost WC5396 London, UK E1 1BR

- Diana, Princess of Wales Memorial Fund, The County Hall, Westminiser Bridge Road, London, UK, SEI78B

- The Great Ormond St. Children's Hospital, London, UK

- Halo Trust, Landmine Victims Support.
  P.O. Box 7712 London, United Kingdom, SWIV3ZA

- National Alliance of Breast Cancer Organization
- 9 E. 37th St., 10th Floor, New York, NY

- National AIDS Trust,
  New City Cloisters 196 Old St., London, UK EC1V9FR

Bibliography/ References

Eide,Rita. The Celestial Voice of Diana; Her Spiritual Guidance to Finding Love.Findhorn Press, 1999, The Park, Findhorn Forres IV363TY, Scotland, UK

The Foundation for Inner Peace. Tiborun, CA.1985.A Course in Miracles. Text, Workbook for Students, Manual for Teachers.

Herman, Cindy.Sound, Movement and Tears: the Natural Way to Release Illness and Stress, Be Loved, be Rich and be Thin, C. 2000, Earthmirth Adventure, Alterfire Publishing, 1835 Oak Terrace, New Castle, CA www.earthmirth.com

Ingram, Julia, Hardin, G.W., The Messengers: A True Story of Angelic Presence and the Return to the Age of Miracles Pocket Books, Division of Simon and Shuster, New York, NY

Jephson, P.D. Shadows of a Princess, An Intimate Account by Her Private Secretary. Harper Collins Publishers 77-85 Fulham Palace Rd., Hammersmith, London, UK W68JB

Kubler-Ross, Elizabeth, 1997 The Wheel of Life: A Memoir of Living and Dying. Simon and Schuster, New York, N.Y.

MacLaine, Shirley. The Camino: A Journey of the Spirit c. 2000 Pocket Books, a Division of Simon and Shuster, New York, NY, London.

MercerPublications.com Mercer, D.M.

Montgomery, Ruth. The World to Come: The Guides Long Awaited Predictions for the Dawning Age.Harmony Books, 201 E. 50th St. New York, NY 10022, Random House Books

Morton, Andrew. Diana, Her True Story. c. 1992. Simon and Shuster, Rockefeller Center 1230 Avenue of the Americas, New York, NY 10020

Murray, Robert. The Stars Still Shine: An Afterlife Journey. Aura Publishing, Derby Line, C.2000,Vermont. www.TheStarsStillShine.com

Pugh, Rev. Rita, Beyond Duality. C. 2001, Truth Beyond Duality, 2002 Lighthouse Publications,

Box 2592 Drumheller, Alberta, Calgary, Canada.

Virtue, Doreen, PhD. Divine Guidance: How to Have a Dialogue With God and Your Guardian Angels, 1998, Renaissance Books, 5858 Wilshire Blvd., Suite 200 Los Angeles, CA 90036

Walsch, Neale Donald. Conversations With God: An Uncommon Dialogue, Book One. 1995.

Hampton Roads Publishing Company, Inc., Charlottesville, VA 22902

Walsch, Neale Donald. Conversations With God; An Uncommon Dialogue, Book Two. 1997

Hampton Roads Publishing Company, Inc. Charlottesville, VA 22902

Walsch, Neale Donald. Conversations With God; an Uncommon Dialogue, Book Three. 1998

Hampton Roads Publishing Company, Inc., Charlottesville, VA 22902

Walsch, Neale Donald. Friendship With God. An Uncommon Dialogue. 1999.J. G. Putnam's Sons, a member of Penguin Putnam, Inc. New York, N.Y. 10014

Webster, Richard. Spirit Guides and Angel Guardians. C 1998, Llwellyn Worldwide, PO Box 64383, St. Paul, MN55164

Appendix

The web site to the book, **Princess Diana's Message of Peace: An Extraordinary Message of Peace for Our World,** by Marcia McMahon, MA is located on the web at:

Diana Speaks to The World

www.dianaspeakstotheworld.com

This website has received much praise from visitors all over the world, and has received a **Margaret's Pages Beautiful Site Award.** To see Diana's recent messages and newer messages from Mother Teresa, go to the site, scroll to the Enter by the Dove, and there you will find the Site Index. Click on any subject you wish from there. Also, on the front page of the web site, you will see at the very bottom of the scroll, the Gallery. To find the magnificent art work in this book, and other Diana paintings, go to the front page of my web site, then go to the word Gallery on the bottom of the scroll. From there, go to Diana Gallery I, 2001 and from there, Diana Gallery II, 2002.

www.dianaspeakstotheworld.com/mb2/diana_speaks/gallery_index.html

I'm always delighted to have visitors on my site and will be happy to hear from you in the Guest book. If you order art work of Princess Diana from the site or this book, be sure to send an email, it is located on the web site.

Web Sites of Note

CNN at **www.cnn.com** CNN gives the latest and best news and has been a major source of news information for this book.

U.S. Department of State, at **www.state.gov/** is an excellent resource to find out what is being done in US world affairs regarding the creation of a Palestine, the war on terror, and diplomatic efforts worldwide, under the direction of the Secretary, Mr. Colin Powell.

United Nations Homepage: **www.un.org/** You may write to the UN and express your concerns over the Iraq situation or the need to create Palestine.

Links To:

Channeling, Spirituality, Princess Diana and other sites:

- Kryon is the entity channeled by LeeCarroll.
- **www.kryon.com/**
- Television Psychics and Mediums UK at (no www)
- **ourworld.compuserve.com/homepages/TVPsychics/**
- Channeling Anthology for September 11, 2001 at:
- **www.spiritwritings.com/september11.html** Princess Diana on 9/11 by Marcia McMahon is

featured here with noted channeling authors, Neale Donald Walsch,

- Annie Kirkwood and R. Murray

The Diana Project,

- **www.users.voicenet.com/~dproject/**
- Princess Diana's Message of Love to Mankind (channeled in French) at
- **www.spiritualendeavors.org/channeling/diana.htm**
- New Beginnings Magazine, by
- **www.spiritual-endeavors.org**
- *Diana, Eternal Voice of Love is featured here
- Angel Diana channeled by Diane Tessman :
- **www3.mistral.co.uk/latrobe/diana.htm**
- Great Dreams:
- **www.greatdreams.com**
- The Charity Work of Princess Diana at
- **www.angelfire.com/ncamberlynn/**
- The Writers Voice, at
- **www.writers-voice.com.**
- (*Princess Diana's Message of Peace, October 26)
- The Stars Still Shine: An Afterlife Journey
- **www.TheStarsStillShine.com**
- Good Works on Earth at
- **http://www.goodworksonearth.org/ladydiana.html** **http://www.goodworksonearth.org/**
- Petals for a Princess, a part of Diana: A Journey Into My Heart at
- **www.angelfire.com /me3/memorial3/**

- The Abbotts Spiritual, New Age and Psychic Site at:
- **www.users.bigpond.com/theabbotts1/section1.htm**

DIANA SPEAKS TO THE WORLD
Web site of Princess Diana's Message of Peace
www.angelfire.com/diana_speaks/gallery_index.html
DIANA GALLERY I AND DIANA GALLERY II

A full color retrospective of all of the watercolors seen in this book and Princess Diana's Message of Peace, II

THE IMMORTAL DIANA: HER STYLE, GRACE and WORDS

A Special Volume of Color Paintings of Princess Diana By Marcia McMahon featuring all her paintings in full glossy color

Announcing the sequel volume of all of Princess Diana's messages, letters to her sons and commentary on diplomatic solutions to the invasion of Iraq plus new revelations in Marcia's forthcoming book! **With Love from Diana, Queen of Hearts, Messages from Heaven for a New Age of Peace, by Marcia McMahon.**

Announcing: ***With Love from Diana, Queen of Hearts***

For a peek inside, Please Go Here:
http://amzn.to/2iJxFeK

www.ingramcontent.com/pod-product-compliance
Lightning Source LLC
LaVergne TN
LVHW051114080426
835510LV00018B/2030

* 9 7 8 0 9 7 6 6 4 7 7 1 3 *